Pestered *by* Plague

The U.S. Public Health Service Station in Astoria, OR and Knappton Cove, WA From Cannery to Quarantine Station 1899–1901

Friedrich E. Schuler

American Humanities Press

Published by American Humanities Press
Portland, Oregon

All rights reserved. No part of this book may be reproduced, stored in a retrieval system or transmitted in any form or by any means—electronic, mechanical, photocopying, recording, or otherwise—without written permission from the copyright owner

Copyright © 2023 by Friedrich E. Schuler.

front cover, top: "Chinamen Filling the Cans"—Interior of a Canning Establishment, Astoria, Oregon. *Clatsop County Historical Society.*
middle: "Dutch sailors aboard deck of the *Utrecht*," published by Bain News Service, *1909. Library of Congress.*
bottom: Mice and rats are presented that were caught on a ship. *National Archives and Records Administration, Washington, D.C.*
back cover, top: Old cannery buildings taken from mast of the ship *Linlithgowshire* before the new Quarantine station was built. *Clatsop County Historical Society.*
middle: A tugboat pulls the *County of Roxborough* to the quarantine station to do ballast excavation. *Columbia River Maritime Museum.*
bottom: The new wharf and buildings built by Leander Lebeck. *Clatsop County Historical Society.*

Layout and cover design: Sam Rascoe, samrascoe@outlook.com

Typefaces used in this book: Century Old Style, Interstate, Minion 3, Proxima Nova

Pestered by Plague: The U.S. Public Health Service Station in Astoria, OR and Knappton Cove, WA, from Cannery to Quarantine Station 1899–1901 / Friedrich E. Schuler. — 1st ed.

ISBN 979-8-218-13250-7

For Colton

Contents

Contents

Acknowledgments

THE GREATEST THANK YOU goes to Nancy Anderson, Heather Henry, and their families. Their loyalty and making space for an additional look at the station remains essential. I am deeply grateful for their support.

The entire board of the Knappton Cove Heritage Museum remains an inspiration. Each tackles some aspect of the museum and, in a vital way, keeps it going. Where would we be without you?

Of course, the National Archives and Records Administration deserves continued praise for preserving our records so we can write a more true history of our nation's institutions. Blessings to the archivists and librarians, insisting that every scrap of paper, eventually, will matter. And they need to be returned, no matter who you are—and teaching that lesson.

An unsung hero of this work is a growing number of individuals working at the Clatsop County Historical Society led by the wonderful McAndrew Burns. Liisa Penner is a treasure and continues to help me think through the history of Astoria's individuals and how they related to the station. I am grateful that Sam Rascoe realized such a magnificent layout. A quiet but very present person is John Goodenberger. Thank you for exchanging insights with me and tolerating my enthusiasm for the station. Jimmy Pearson at the public library of Astoria needs to be added as equal to Liisa Penner and John Goodenberger. Those three are my good spirits, deeply caring about the city and the material that contains its story. And they make it available every day!

In Portland, a thank you goes to Prof. Dr. John Ott, the Chair of the History Department at Portland State University and one of the great historians of medieval worlds in our country. Every author should have the luck to experience his encouragement, help, and the space he provides.

Thank you to Francheska Cannone for editing the draft text. The entire PSU Department of History continues to provide a life-of-the-mind environment, resisting never ceasing efforts of becoming shallow or just simply uneducated in a new way.

Every station should have a chaplain. David Knapp—no pun intended—has consistently given true spiritual encouragement. One day he will tell us how closely his family's name is related to the region.

The thank you section would not be complete without mentioning former chief Tim Garrison.

Julia, Vienna, Mave, and Colton remain my favorites. Colton, what a joy it is to dedicate this book to you. Hopefully, one day, you will write one too.

The most important thank you to Silke for sharing history so deeply, joyfully, and for sixteen years! A very lucky man I am, indeed. Life has become a never-ending history seminar. Which archive are we going to next? Yipee!

Did I mention United Airlines, which provides such magnificent long-distance flights that allow for perfect concentration?

INTRODUCTION

THIS BOOK TELLS HOW PLAGUE, not COVID-19, threatened Astoria, Oregon. The plague scare from 1899 to 1900 defined the work environment of the first United States Public Health Service assistant surgeon Dr. Hill Hastings after he was sent to the mouth of the Columbia River to transform a mothballed cannery building into the first unit of a yet-to-be-built larger federal quarantine complex. Of course, this story is also about the difference a doctor's leadership makes when quarantine work moves from thinking and talking about health to action among people. The cannery's transformation was realized during the West Coast's most serious public health crisis before the 1918 Spanish Flu epidemic. Dr. Hastings mastered it as the first of many unique, noteworthy doctors of the USPHS out of his office on Commercial Street, Astoria, and the new fumigation buildings and hospital at Knappton Cove, WA.

VIEW OF ASTORIA, OREGON. CA. 1885.

[1]

From the Outset: A Challenging Assignment

ON APRIL 28, 1899, at the United States Public Health Service[1] in Seattle, Dr. Hill Hastings received the order to relocate to the mouth of the Columbia River, the second-largest river in the United States.[2] He arrived in Astoria, Oregon, on Tuesday, May 9th. His task was to open a quarantine station on the Washington side of the river and manage and operate it out of his small office at 511 Commercial Street. That meant converting a former cannery near Knappton, Washington, into a building for public health. In the future, there, crews should be bathed, and passengers screened and vaccinated. Also, disinfection of suitcases, cargo, ships, and ballast might take place. Finally, Hastings should hire staff to perform the fumigation and disinfection.

On the day of his arrival, Dr. Hastings asked Customs Collector John Fox to ferry him across the bay to see with his own eyes the mothballed wooden buildings.[3] Afterward, he performed his first public relations act. He announced that he was pleased with what he saw:

---

[1] Until 1903 this service was called United States Marine Service. Thereafter it became the United States Public Health Service. From here on I use the abbreviation USPHS.

[2] National Library of Medicine, United States Public Health Service Weekly Report, Vol. XIV, No. 20, May 19, 1899 (hereafter cited as USPHS Report 1899.)

[3] Astoria, OR, Astoria Public Library, *Astoria Daily Budget*, May 9, 1899, "About the City."[hereafter cited as ADB].

DR. HILL HASTINGS.

> *this bay and these buildings were an admirable location for the erection of a disinfection plant. In front of the buildings plenty of deep water flowed in the channel and abundant water from a stream nearby would satisfy the technical requirements of cleaning ships out but also treat crews and passengers.*[4]

After crossing back to Astoria, Hastings might have even met the cannery's former owner, Hume, in town. Hume had not yet received payment for the real estate sale. Was it only a coincidence that he arrived in Astoria the same day as Dr. Hastings?[5] The truth was that across the bay in Washington stood a building in legal and financial limbo.

Until now, Dr. Jay Tuttle had corresponded with the U.S. Department of Treasury. His private practice was located at 477 Commercial Street.

He was born in 1841 in Nottingham, New Hampshire, and graduated from the New Hampshire Philipps Exeter Academy. Once he arrived in Oregon, he served from 1874 to 1876 as Sheriff of Coos Bay. Next, he worked as a Demonstrator of Anatomy for four years at Willamette University's Medical Department. Once he graduated from the same university with an M.D. degree, he was hired by Astoria's St. Mary's Hospital as a physician and surgeon. Four years before Hill Hastings arrived, in 1885, Dr. Tuttle opened his private practice in Astoria at 477 Commercial Street.[6] His private residence was located at 639 Exchange Street and gave him and his family the luxury of eight bedrooms.[7]

During the entire time, he worked for the federal government taking care of issues pertaining to the U.S. Marine Hospital Service, including dealing with the bills of health handed to

[4] *ADB*, May 10, 1899, "About the City."
[5] *ADB*, May 9, 1899, "About the City."
[6] NLM, Association of Military Surgeons of the United States, Personal Records of Members, General History, 1901. Jay Tuttle. Here his private residence is listed incorrectly as Commercial St. 477.
[7] The residence had baths and steel ranges.

him by captains of recently arrived ships.[8] Still, Dr. Tuttle's main job was that of a city physician. Now, in May 1899, Dr. Hastings assumed command over Dr. Tuttle. From then on, Dr. Hastings would be the main USPHS physician inspecting incoming foreign ships and passengers.

The Astoria of 1899 was different from the Astoria tourists experience today. If Hastings thought that one could tie up an ocean-going vessel at the city's wharf, he quickly learned that no deep channel for an ocean-going vessel existed. "Making the channel deeper" was a well-familiar refrain. Even that was easier said than done. The workers hired to deepen the area in front of the railroad O&R railroad tracks dug as deep as their hand tools allowed. In June 1899, it was decided to use dynamite right in front of the railroad trestle to blow through the layer of clay to make the spot in front of the railroad deep enough for an ocean-going vessel.[9]

Nobody in town owned a car. However, one hundred bicycles were licensed. At the same time, in Portland, people rode 3,900 bicycles more.[10] Astorians also owned one hundred dogs, but ninety citizens refused to take out a canine city license. For Clatsop County, the fishing commission issued 1,798 fishing licenses to individuals, 821 gillnet licenses, two seine licenses, and three trap licenses.[11] The largest salmon caught would measure four feet and four inches and weigh eighty-one and one-half pounds.[12]

The city was more cut off from the world than one might imagine. Only the best hotel in town, the Occident Hotel, had recently acquired a long-distance telephone line.[13] The rest of the communication was realized by many competing telegraph stations. West of Astoria, the city was still cut off from Warrenton as the construction of a bridge remained to be finished any month now.

[8] *ADB*, June 5, 1900, "About the City."
[9] *ADB*, June 19, 1899, "About the City."
[10] *ADB*, April 28, 1899 and *ADB*, June 4, 1899, "About the City."
[11] Ibid., May 7, 1899," "About the City."
[12] Ibid., May 30, 1899, "About the City."
[13] Astoria's best hotel, Hotel Occident acquired on April 29, 1899 one long distance line. *ADB* 4, 28, 1899, "About the City."

And yet, one could look at an original Spanish war flag in town. Most recently, Charles Clase ripped it out of the hands of a Spaniard in the Philippines.[14] The main entertainment was minstrel shows that regularly toured the entire region. Regularly, ships from South America, especially Peru and Chile, docked at Astoria's wharf, and coal was imported from Australia.

Politically speaking, a major issue in town was the future availability of electric-powered lights. Sixty streetlights burned in town and one in front of city hall. At that time, electricity for the bulbs was supplied by the West Shore Mill, owned by members of the Trullinger family. Now, the West Shore Mill wanted to sign a new contract for fifty lights at the cost of $375.[15] Hill Hastings's tenure in town coincided with the beginning of a slow but steady move toward an electricity boycott by members of the Trullinger family. Such was the quirky, serious, and more dangerous than necessary context for Hill Hastings's appearance in the summer of 1899.

How does one convert a cannery into a quarantine station? There existed no comparable transformation in the U. S. that Dr. Hastings could study. A lot was common sense. He had to find carpenters who could construct shower rooms. He had to find handymen willing to fit pipes where before salmon had been stuffed into cans. He had to install boilers and fire them up to make steam until it mixed with sulfur into a dangerous vapor, ready to penetrate and fill a ship's hull to kill invisible microbes. Also, he had to find a guaranteed supply of potable water. Without it, a ship could not be fumigated, nor could passengers receive their bath or shower.

And yet, Dr. Hastings preferred to think about his future in Astoria in terms of what would come after next year's transformation of the cannery. Then, near Knappton, a federally managed USPHS Hospital would hopefully get built near the fumigation building. Hastings imagined not just one quarantine building but an *entire* complex consisting of several buildings performing

[14] Ibid., May 28, 1899, "About the City."
[15] Ibid., May 4, 1899, "About the City."

differentiated tasks, all serving public health needs in Washington and Oregon. Hastings's 1900 to-do list included just the first most essential tasks.

Most observers were unaware that Dr. Hastings was sent to Astoria and Knappton to keep commerce flowing during a pandemic—but not to shut the trade down. With modest means and hardly any help, he was to make possible the impossible. He was not to act as a gatekeeper who locked or unlocked the mouth of the river based on his personal evaluation. Instead, he was to be a public health problem solver, always assuming that the exchange of goods on the river had to continue despite the coming and going of dangerous diseases or an infected crew. Most Astorians insisted on the continued movements of goods and an economy that earned Oregonians and wealthy outsiders an income. Shutting down the Columbia River was unfathomable for Astorian elites.

Dr. Hastings, opening his office, room 601, inside the old Spexarth building at 511 Commercial Street, pulled off a flying start. On his third day in town, the *SS Columbia* arrived carrying 330 passengers. Previously, most of them crossed the Pacific. From Japan, 230 traveled in steerage. Before reaching Hawaii, the *SS Columbia's* health officer wired the presence of one passenger ill with smallpox. But then, this diseased man was taken off the vessel in Honolulu. The ship continued to Astoria, as far as anybody could tell, without the appearance of another virulent case on board.

Nevertheless, once the *SS. Columbia* dropped its anchor into the bay, Dr. Hastings examined all 330 individuals on board to confirm that, indeed, this was a ship free of smallpox. Fortunately, he did not find a new case.

Next, he checked the vaccination status of everyone. Unvaccinated crew and passengers received a shot in the arm on location whether they wanted to or not. Afterward, Hastings ordered all cabins to be fumigated where passengers slept coming

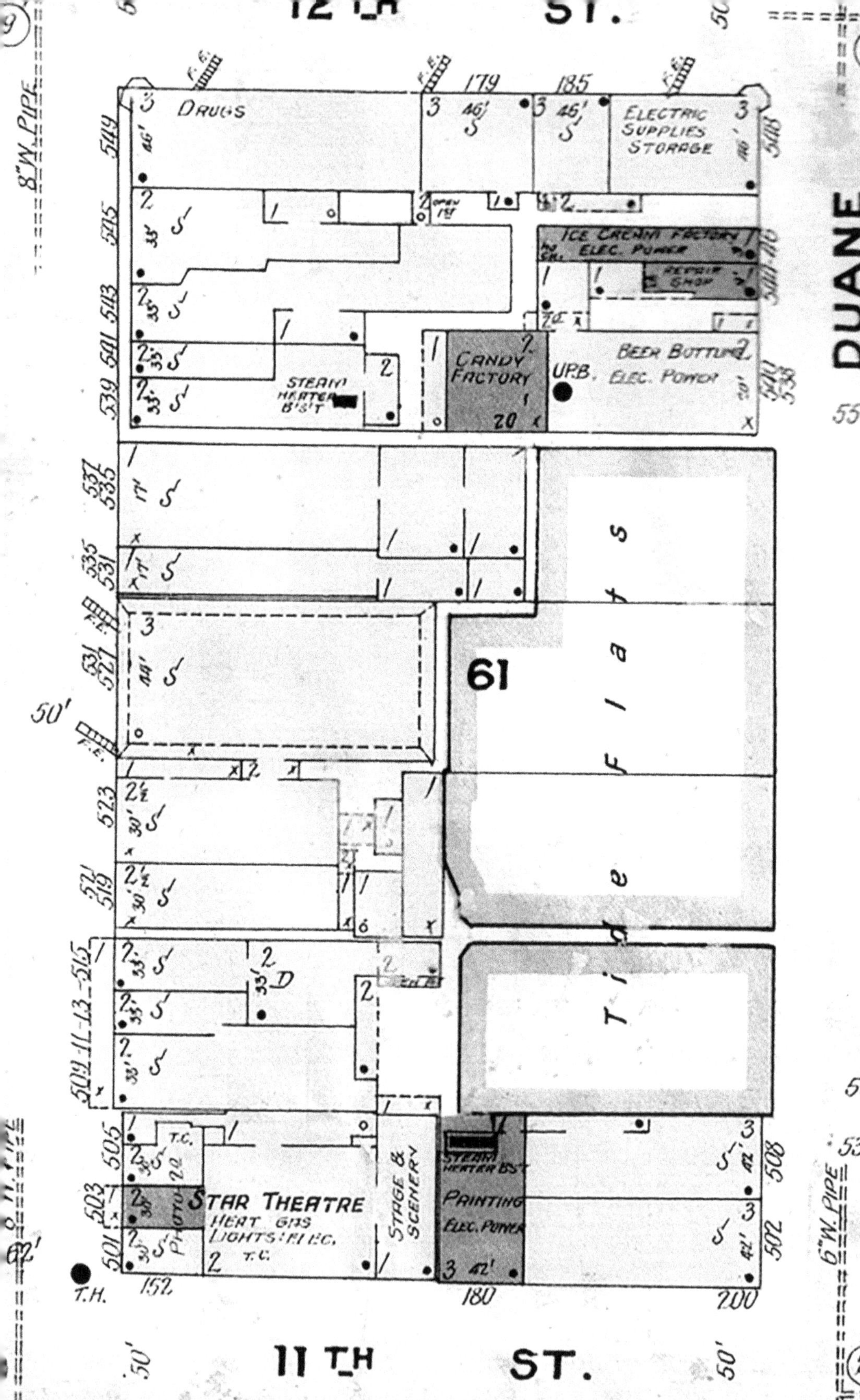

12TH ST.
DRUGS
ELECTRIC SUPPLIES STORAGE
ICE CREAM FACTORY
ELEC. POWER
REPAIR SHOP
CANDY FACTORY
BEER BOTTLING
ELEC. POWER
STEAM HEATER B'S'T
DUANE
61
Tide Flats
STAR THEATRE
HEAT GAS
LIGHTS: ELEC.
PHOTO
STAGE & SCENERY
STEAM HEATER BST
PAINTING
ELEC. POWER
8" W. PIPE
6" W. PIPE
T.H.
152
180
200
11TH ST.

from mainland Asia.[16] Finally, he asked that all the luggage be opened, and he fumigated it too. Later that week, because the cannery building across the bay could not yet be used, Hastings opened a temporary emergency disinfection and fumigation site on a wharf in Astoria.[17]

In Astoria, serious diseases short of plague did circulate in 1899, and inhabitants lived with that reality. Anybody visiting for social or business reasons could run into somebody suffering from tuberculosis, polio, or syphilis. Regularly there was diphtheria in homes. In April 1899, smallpox was arriving again. From East Portland, it spread into the Northwest, advancing toward Astoria. People simply lived on expecting its arrival. They neither stopped their lives nor let it interrupt their work. They prayed and made their own choices on how to relate to diseases. Besides, what could one really do against them in 1899? No effective medicines and only a few weak vaccines existed.

After the *SS Columbia's* arrival, the *SS Monmouthshire* came from Hong Kong. Dr. Hastings again checked people for quarantinable diseases and found none, but he still fumigated the suitcases. In particular, he was determined to kill any virus coming from Hong Kong expected to be plague or cholera.[18] Previously on July 8, 1899, the *SS Lenox* brought news that in Hong Kong, 204 deaths resulted from bubonic plague.[19] At the end of June, Dr. Hastings learned that the *Nippon Maru*, traveling from Hong Kong to Honolulu, reported one passenger dying from plague. When the *Nippon Maru* reached San Francisco, it was quarantined right away at Angel Island, and 379 passengers and the vessel were disinfected. Surprisingly, two stowaways crawled out of the poisonous sulfur fog escaping from the ship's hull. Then they jumped into the frigid ocean water of San Francisco Bay. Fortunately, they

16 *ADB*, May 19 1899, "About the City."
17 *ADB*, May 17, 1899, "About the City."
18 National Archives and Records Administration (hereafter cited as NARA,) Washington, D.C., RG 90, "Letter," Hill Hastings to Supervising General, D.C. , June 1899.
19 Ibid., "*Electric*", "Letter, Hastings to Supervising Surgeon General, July 3, 1899.

LOCATION, ASTORIA OFFICE OF USPHS,
COMMERCIAL STREET. CA. 1900.

were caught before the cold water could kill them, or they could carry any undiscovered disease into the city. Still, this *Nippon Maru* incident made news up and down the U. S. West Coast and circulated in Astoria's maritime circles. The incident hinted at the increasing possibility that U. S. health officials could experience the arrival of plague in the very, very near future. It appeared to be not just plausible but likely.

Dr. Hastings, too, feared that one case of plague would break through the defensive parameters the USPHS erected in the 1820s. Plague in Astoria would be a true catastrophe, he knew. Astoria remained isolated. Only since this year, 1899, did a railroad track connect Astoria with the world and offer a reliable half-day trip out of town to escape. Otherwise, everything and everybody but fish, milk, and beef were brought in by boat. Large stern-wheelers needed almost a day's trip to reach Portland. Knappton, opposite of Astoria, would not be connected with a paved all-weather road until 1936.[20] In Astoria, not a single person owned a car until 1903.

Further north, the new reliable bridge crossing Young's Bay was just finished. In case of a health panic, who knew if people in Warrenton would not pull up the bridge and force Astorians to swim across Youngs bay or, at least, paddle their own boat? In one day, doctors and nurses could have arrived from Portland if they chose to work with plague. It would have taken a few days longer from Seattle by sea or rail. From San Francisco, a trip would have taken almost a week.

Just as troubling was the absence of a local federal laboratory set aside to examine potentially infected specimens safely. In essence, Astorians would have to resort to lockdowns in town with hardly any way out. Self-quarantine was all there was. Initially, they would have to rely on each other. Unclear was who would guarantee the safe transport of a seriously infected person. To consider economic and employment consequences seemed not to have occurred to anybody. No written plan existed. The outcome

[20] WA, Carlton E. Appelo, *Knappton the first 50 years*, Pacific County, 1975.

of a plague outbreak was made more terrifying due to the lack of the most basic regional or local planning. In elite circles, the prevailing feeling was that it would be really appreciated if Dr. Hastings, somehow, could catch the one case that might sneak past inspectors in Canton, Hong Kong, Kobe, Honolulu, Rio, Lisbon, or even San Francisco. So that people would not be ripped out of their life plans and certainties they so appreciated and took for granted.

[2]

Before Hill Hastings's Tenure: Astoria's Local Medical Community Does or Does Not Engage Incoming Diseases From Abroad

DR. HASTINGS WAS NOT the first to operate a public health system in Astoria. Initially, a federal office at the old post office existed. Dr. Tuttle gave the USPHS a better and more steady local presence there. Most importantly, Tuttle established cooperation with Oregon's public health office in Astoria. Dr. Hastings's arrival represented only an additional national presence. Hastings entered a decade-old state run public health environment staffed by select Astorian doctors.

Until Dr. Hastings's arrival, ships, crews, passengers, and cargo experienced, on occasion, public inspection on the city's wharf conducted by Dr. A. C. Fulton, the most recent State of Oregon Health Officer for Astoria. Whenever Dr. Tuttle went out of town, he made it a habit to appoint Dr. Fulton as a stand-in for the USPHS. If necessary, Fulton and Tuttle ordered a ship to sail to an anchor place near Tongue Point and await further orders. When they steamed toward a ship, they were ferried by

DR. A.C. FULTON.

Domingo Besserich; an Austrian immigrant hired as a boatman for the State's Health Office of Astoria. [21]

Dr. Fulton, undoubtedly, was the stronger and more influential of the two. He could draw on significant social power as he was one of a group of brothers who held key political positions in the city and Oregon's Legislature in Salem, Oregon. Dealing with Dr. Fulton always meant dealing with a family that counted as its member, the Oregon Senate president and head of the Republican Party.

A third brother was Chas W. Fulton, a lawyer. He incorporated some of Astoria's most successful large businesses, sometimes financed by national investors. C. W. Fulton incorporated the Epicure Fish Company and the Washington Mercantile Company. Later, he was secretary of the Astoria company that lumber baron Hammond incorporated in New Jersey.[22] In 1906 C. W. Fulton served as Vice President of Finance of the Astoria and Columbia River Railroad (A&CR). Of course, he, too, was a member of the Republican party. Another brother was George Clyde Fulton, who, in 1899, presided over Astoria's Rowing Club and served as chairman of the Astoria Regatta. In 1900 he gave Pendleton's 4th of July speech. This was a very well-connected political family with regional prominence and power.[23]

Dr. Fulton did not wield power directly or openly. It might impress people that he previously attended clinics in Vienna, Berlin, London, and Edinburg.[24] Also, he served as overseer of Astoria's poor farm in 1890. That did not bring riches, only a yearly pay of $1,000.[25] However, Dr. Fulton was well enough off

[21] *ADB*, May 24, 1900, "About the City."
[22] *ADB*, May 8, 1899, "About the City."
[23] Ibid., May 31, 1899, "About the City." Being so well connected also meant that people asked him to speak publicly. For example in 1899 he was the Memorial Day speaker for Astoria.
[24] Astoria, Clatsop County History Society, Folder: Fulton. In 1902 he would give a presentation on appendicitis. He was a member of the Oregon State Medical Society.(Hereafter cited as CCHS).
[25] Before Fulton in 1890 O.B. Estes had held a position called Quarantine Officer of the Port of Astoria.

to vacation in Paso Robles, California.[26] He was an important and well-liked doctor in town. Obviously, people had deeper bonds with him than with Dr. Hastings, but Fulton could not marshal federal law.

In 1899 nothing dramatic was reported about the work Dr. Fulton and Dr. Tuttle performed regarding quarantine services. To everybody's relief, federal U. S. health representatives stationed abroad still successfully realized most of the passenger and crew screenings. Most often, at the end of a ship's journey Drs. Fulton or Tuttle awaited the captain, in hand a bill of health that certified a ship and crew as disease free. The two performed well in the role everybody expected them to perform.

Just as important was that they did not get into anybody's way in town. No records suggest that they ever sued a captain for refusing to follow procedures. They did not go too far, act dictatorial, or tell Astorians, city dignitaries, or chamber of commerce committees how to conduct their business. After Dr. Hastings arrived, the state health officer, the USPHS representative, and city leaders coexisted comfortably within productive social and professional arrangements. There was a distinct Astorian medical community functioning with local and regional ties that Dr. Hastings was expected to respect. And he did.

Hill Hastings traveled hundreds of miles from Seattle to Astoria only to realize that the last two miles from Astoria's wharf to incoming ships remained difficult to breach. The key task of the new USPHS head was to step onto a launch at Astoria's wharf and steam toward an incoming foreign ship. Once reached, he would board it and, finally, have the legal power to insist that captains followed the federal code of health covering crew, passengers, cargo, and ballast. Surprisingly, Dr. Hastings's tenure began without any mode of water transportation of his own. His first, most pressing problem was obtaining reliable and predictable water transportation. Also, only a ship would enable Hastings to

[26] Astoria Library, ADB, May 11, 1899 "About the City."

travel across the bay and reach the station where, in the future, diseased passengers and crews would wait or heal.

To make matters more challenging, he had to transform a mothballed wooden building that was not yet safe into one where public health could be practiced. In his first year, he might discover on ships men or women with diseases, but in his first year, he had no building to isolate them. What he did have was an excellent medical education, good practical work experience, a uniform, national contacts, an office on Commercial Street, and real federal legal power that ranked above Oregon law and Astoria's local customs. He had to rely on Astoria's medical community. Fortunately for him, Astoria's leadership wanted him to succeed as long as his work did not reduce their income.

WISE'S CLEAN SWEEP SALE
TELEGRAPH
Telegraph-Cable Co
THE COFFMAN
Furnished Rooms
BANK

[3]

First Tools: Securing a Boat and Building

DR. HASTINGS THOUGHT ABOUT all of this in room 601 inside his office at 511 Commercial Street.[27] His transformation of the cannery at Knappton began with asserting legal ownership over the building. That was easier said than done. It meant asking the U. S. Department of Justice to certify in writing that the building's legal new ownership was recorded correctly.[28] Hastings knew it would take months before he could hold the desired official deed in his hands. It was annoying how little Washington, D. C.'s bureaucracy, in 1899, cared about bringing the Astoria station online. In May, one source suggested that the title was last seen at the office of Oregon's district attorney. Others thought it was kept in an attorney's office in Seattle. When letters were written asking to find out where the title was currently located, no written answer was returned.[29] Dr. Hastings could only look across the bay and observe the buildings, but he could not yet nail into place the shower benches for passengers nor install chambers to fumigate clothes. His was the most frustrating situation.

Dr. Hastings was impatient. And so, on Saturday, June 24, 1899, he and a few carpenters crossed the Columbia River and docked

[27] Astoria City and Clatsop County Directory, Also a Directory of the Towns of Pacific and Wahkiakum Counties, Wash. 1904, Vol. III (Portland, OR: R. L. Polk & CO., 1904) page 16, entry for U.S. Quarantine Station. Clatsop County Historical Society's Internet Archive, City Directories Collection. (https://archive.org/details/astoriacitydirectory.1904/page/16/mode/2up?q=Quarantine+Station: accessed November 21, 2022)

[28] Washington, D. C., Library of Congress, (hereafter cited as LOC), Chronicling America, Newspapers, Oregon, Astoria Morning, October 13, 1899.

[29] *ADB*, May 17, 1899, "About the City."

1900 ASTORIA USPHS OFFICE, COMMERCIAL STREET 511, ROOM 601.

at the cannery's old wharf. After unlocking the door, they walked through the interior full of tables and conveyor belts previously used to prepare salmon for canning.[30] These notes became the basis for prioritizing future construction tasks and to provide cost estimates to be mailed to Washington, D. C. Three weeks later, in August, Hastings held, in hand, proposals detailing repairs valued to cost $15,000.00. The proposal imagined one new wharf for $10,500, a new barrack on shore for $9,000, the general repair of existing buildings costing $10,000, and replacing the old approach on shore for $2,000. Additional items mentioned but not yet priced out where: heat stoves, light oil lamps, and tents for the exceptional situation that 1,000 to 1,200 people needed to be cared for.[31] For Hastings, these items detailed phase one only.

He dreamed of building additional buildings in the future: one additional hospital barrack, two barracks for immigrants sized 120x30 feet to house 350 people; a second building for seventy-five people sized 40x30 feet; a hospital building for ten people measuring 40x20 feet; a pest house building to quarantine people with contagious diseases only. All would be built close to the Columbia River. Knappton would remain the exclusive place to operate a quarantine station.[32] Holding this proposal in hand, Hastings hoped that in Washington, D. C., U. S. Surgeon General Wyman would feel like endorsing it and win senators willing to appropriate such funds.

Hastings's effort to secure a ship succeeded faster.[33] Already on his fifth day in Astoria, from Washington, D. C., the USPHS ordered him to find a shipyard in Astoria that could build a boat for the exclusive use of the federal government's public health service.[34] In theory, this order helped Dr. Hastings because it described the path the government wanted him to take. However, it solved little since it would take at least half a year to build such

[30] Ibid., June 25, 1899, "About the City."
[31] Astoria, Astoria Public Library, APL 00025, Dr. Leinassar Collection, Box 1 of 1.
[32] Ibid.
[33] Often wharf 39 was used.
[34] *ADB*, May 29, 1899, "About the City."

BACK OF BUILDING 1905, ECHOES OF BEING A CANNERY.

a boat. But how should he approach incoming vessels until an Astorian shipyard constructed such a launch?

Until then, Dr. Hastings could only rent a small ship. But still, even that was easier said than done. As he walked from boat owner to boat owner, asking about availability and rental cost, he always heard the same answer: all suitable tugs were either busy or under contract. It was salmon harvesting season, after all.

Eventually, it was again U. S. Collector of Customs, John Fox, who helped Dr. Hastings to find a ship. Fox told Hastings about the owner-operator Captain W. W. Babbidge. He owned a launch called *Electric*. It was an older ship built in 1885 for Captain A. C. Fisher. Then it was sold to Charles Gunderson and Thomas Russell. After that, Captain Babbidge bought it to operate a run on the Skippanon River and to sort logs. In 1895 it needed partial rebuilding.[35] In 1899 its boiler needed attention. John Fox also praised Babbidge as one of Astoria's best pilots, intimately knowing the waters of the dangerous Columbia bar.

Dr. Hastings located Babbidge, began negotiations, and, at first, experienced sticker shock: Babbidge wanted $600 rent per month. That amount would pay for the boat, the crew and fuel. Hastings countered by asking to charter the boat only but not a package that included crew and fuel. His orders were to spend only $200. He was to hire a crew himself and find cheaper fuel.[36] Hastings should offer wages of ninety dollars per month for the captain, ninety dollars per month for the engineer, and fifty dollars per month for a deckhand.[37] Hastings hired the *Electric* for several weeks during contract negotiations on a per-trip basis. The price per voyage was five dollars.[38]

---

[35] Astoria, Astoria Public Library, APL 00025, Dr. Leinassar Collection, Box 1 of 1.

[36] NARA, RG 90, Hastings to supervising surgeon general of the Maritime Hospital office, "letter," May 12, 1899.

[37] NARA, RG 90, "*Electric*" files, Hastings to Washington, D. C., "letter," May 12, 1899 and June 10, 1899.

[38] The cost was five dollars per trip, NARA, RG 90, Hastings, "letter," May 24, 1899.

MANY USPHS DOCTORS DREAMED OF LEADING LARGE HOSPITALS LIKE THIS ONE; NOT A SMALL LAZARETTO AS IN KNAPPTON.

For four weeks, Hastings and Babbidge talked back and forth. Hastings insisted on minor changes to convert the *Electric* into a vessel able to perform quarantine work. Second, he wanted installed ventilators and a storage place to transport an emergency disinfection apparatus. Plus, Babbidge was asked to learn the federal rules of quarantine. On June 10, 1899, Dr. Hastings and Captain Babbidge signed a contract covering three months from June 10 to October 10.[39] How transportation should be realized thereafter, Hastings did not know. Still, no plans to build a ship had been made, nor had Dr. Hastings approached local shipyards. Certainly, his dependency on local boat owners would continue in 1900.

Immigration processing was also part of Dr. Hastings's duties. However, behind the word immigration stands a very complex reality. And the availability of limited sources might ask us to reserve final judgment until we have conclusive evidence. However, a good, educated guess can be ventured. Astoria never was a major U.S. port of entry for people who wanted to move to the U.S. and become citizens. Those interested in becoming U.S. citizens crossed the oceans on the great transpacific shipping lines. Their West Coast terminuses were San Francisco, Port Townsend, Tacoma, Seattle, or Victoria in British Columbia. Therefore, the number of immigrants in Astoria compared to major U.S. East and West coast cities was tiny. We know exactly how many immigrants walked by Dr. Hill Hastings and showed him their papers. On September 2nd, 1899, the records say Hastings processed fifty "Japanese immigrants."[40] If we compare the August number of fifty immigrants coming through Astoria with the 20,746 coming through New York in August 1899, the difference between the Ellis Island of New York and our little wharf with a disinfection building becomes apparent. In September 1899, Dr. Hastings processed another eighteen people, this time called "Japanese aliens."[41] This adds up to a total of sixty-eight people for the year 1899.

[39] In the end it was Babbidge who put together a crew.
[40] USPHS weekly report, Vol. XIV, September 1899.
[41] Ibid., October 1899.

The issue of examining individuals arriving in Astoria deserves, however, further differentiation. Astoria was a major port for individuals who came short term for labor purposes during salmon season. Thousands of Chinese contract laborers and Finnish sailors must have walked by somebody. However, this was not the doctor of the USPHS. Surviving records indicate that in Astoria, contract laborers were handled by the U. S. customs service, more precisely, its deputy director. I would venture that only if a contract laborer was visibly ill might Dr. Hastings have become involved.

The surviving paperwork complicates finding quick, definitive answers. The racism of the 19th century created policies that differentiated Asian immigrants—the Chinese exclusion act, in particular, separated Asian immigrants by ethnicity. Thus, a single form was used for people arriving from Japan. On the other hand, Chinese individuals hardly ever appear with an identity on one separate sheet of paper. Their names and origin were, most likely, recorded by their Chinese labor contractor, who led the arriving laborers into Astoria's work setting as if they were a bulk commodity. Thus, when Hastings processed Japanese "immigrants" or "aliens," he might have also processed agricultural or seasonal Japanese fishery workers.

Finally, in our popular culture, all too often, the USPHS is suspected of, somehow, being abusive and using its federal power to discriminate against Asian immigrants. Since we have an exact record of people being shown to Dr. Hastings, we can check how discriminating his decisions were. Easily, as he stood alone on Astoria's dock, he could have conjured up some existing or non-existing malady forcing the Chinese or Japanese person to return home. Dr. Hastings rejected precisely zero individuals of all fifty people he examined. He passed all immigrants or aliens. As far as immigration was concerned in his first year at Astoria, Dr. Hastings, the representative of the USPHS and the federal government, did not abuse the power of examination, period. Later, when we deal with his work in 1900, we should ask the same again. Then we can judge Hastings's behavior during his entire tenure.

[4]
Adding Federal Procedure to Local Custom

ON THE SAME DAY after signing the contract for the *Electric*, Dr. Hastings staged a public demonstration. He announced to Astoria's maritime and business community that he and the U. S. government were able and willing to impose rules onto Oregon quarantine laws and local tradition. He sent messages to administrators, stevedores, bar pilots, and freight managers that any vessel potentially carrying a foreign disease must first be stopped and then examined by Dr. Hastings and his aids. Until then, no other Astorian should get close. If necessary, ships would be fumigated even if that prolonged their journey by two days. Only after Dr. Hastings had cleared the ship would it be passed on to longshoremen to unload cargo or guide it up the Columbia River toward Portland.[42]

Dr. Hastings used the arrival of the *SS Columbia* on June 10, 1899, to make his point. In the afternoon, he boarded the *Electric* and approached the *SS Columbia*. Interestingly, Hastings asked Oregon's health officer, Dr. J. A. Fulton, to accompany him on the trip.

Dr. Hastings had reason to be concerned about the *SS Columbia*. It started in Hong Kong and continued to Yokohama, Japan. Before reaching Japan, her captain reported that one passenger

[42] We are lacking a description if, when and how Oregon's health representative fumigated incoming ocean vessels before June 1899. A 1915 report states that there had existed a facility on the Astorian side that was available when necessary. See NARA, Seattle, Quarantine Station files, Report 1915.

SS Columbia. ca. 1900–1907.

"	" Ken	-	-	-	-	$20

E. & O. E.

Yokohama 19th October 1899.

DODWELL & Co., Limited.

[signature]
Sub-Manager.

Columbia River Quarantine Station, Astoria, Oregon,

...ssioner of Immigration, Portland,

I certify to having given each of the above named alien ... examination to determine their fitness for entrance to the U... no one is suffering from such disease or injury that ... ...lude under the Immigration Laws.

was suspected of being ill, showing signs of valaroid—a scientific term hiding the disease of plague. Then, in Yokohama, this passenger was asked to leave the ship and quarantined in Japan. Thus, the *SS Columbia's* captain could hand Hastings a clean bill of health.

Until May 1899, a captain presenting such a clean bill of health would have received clearance. However, in June 1899, on a Friday afternoon, Hastings modeled what needed to be improved in the future. The next day he investigated her passengers and her crew. No one was permitted to leave her or board her. Then, he checked all for vaccinations and vaccinated those who had no proof of having received one. After that, he fumigated *SS Columbia's* steerage quarters. Only after all this work was finished could the *SS Columbia* venture back onto the river and continue. From then on, such federal procedure had to be followed 100% of the time. Otherwise, this federal representative would fine violators regardless of how well they were connected to Astoria and her traditions.

After this demonstration, Dr. Hastings invaded the autonomy of Astoria's tug pilots. On August 8, 1899, new federal regulations amended quarantine rules in domestic ports. From then on, tugboats contacting ships that may potentially be carrying diseases had to follow Hastings's protocol.

People took note that the leader of a quarantine station could change the commercial rhythm of the bay. New rhythms were a two-day wait to realize the inspection of their papers, cargo, and passengers. Subsequently, quarantine could keep a ship sequestered for two weeks. If a ship's ballast also had to be changed, the waiting time could be four weeks.

DR. HASTINGS' NOTE TO PORTLAND COMMISSIONER OF IMMIGRATION, NOVEMBER 1899.

[5]

Megalomaniacal Entrepreneurial Distractions

BY THE FALL OF 1899, Dr. Hastings learned of another power impacting Astoria's daily life: the dreams and actions of entrepreneur A. B. Hammond. Like an eagle frequently circling over a territory, A. B. Hammond's aura hovered over the city. Most recently, he had brought the railroad to Astoria and, thus, was celebrated as the pinnacle of Astoria's leading economic, social and political scene. Still, he did not live among Astorians. Nor did he seem to have the desire to do so. His office remained in Portland, and he preferred to live in San Francisco, California. His only effort to be more connected to Astoria was the laying of a direct telephone line from his Portland office in the *Oregonian* building to his Astorian representative.[43]

As he "circled" over Clatsop County, he discerned new market opportunities. He had unrivaled energy generating, renewing hope for a richer Astorian commercial future and expanding economic greed without asking who would pay the price. In January 1899, he was a key player in the reorganization of the city's salmon fishing industry. At the Occident Hotel, Hammond's

[43] LOC, Chronicling America, *Morning Astorian*, September 12, 1899. Compared to the Hammonds, the families of Van Dusens, Trullingers, Kinneys, Elmores, and Fultons were perceived as living a social rank beneath. That he used them and their influence was painfully obvious, even though that also meant they could profit selectively from Hammond's exploitation. At the same time, Hammond was painfully aware that his power, too, depended on huge investments of East Coast investors and especially the Huntington family which socially ranked higher than he did. These national investors also inspired the expectations of Astoria's leading families.

ANDREW B. HAMMOND.

private secretary Gosslin announced a new capitalization of the salmon industry worth one million dollars. Newspaper readers were told that such industrial concentration would guarantee the employment of 4,000 workers. In typical Hammond fashion he failed to explain what that would mean for the life of the average Astorian and the fish.[44]

A. B. Hammond inspired some a second time when at the end of March 1899, Mr. Finley, a timber cruiser, identified 6,000 acres of trees between Seaside and Nehalem, Oregon. This news was interpreted as Hammond wishing to extend the Astoria Columbia Railroad down the coast.

Hammond inspired or scared people a third time when he held out the prospect of acquiring a lumber mill in Astoria. Also, Hammond's former partner Hathaway wanted to acquire a mill. Already, the Trullingers reported that interested parties looked at their West Shore Mill. [45] Importantly, Hammond pointed to events in Albany, Oregon. There, leading citizens donated land so that investors felt like financing the construction of a huge lumber mill. A year ago, he demanded large amounts of land from Astorian elites to bring the railroad to the port. Now, Hammond wanted some of Astoria's best shoreland to bring a huge mill to the city.

Hammond deflected any doubts with more extravagant dreams. He dangled in front of Astoria's leading families the intoxicating prospect that, anytime now, he would open a new steamship line running directly between San Francisco and Astoria. Already the year before, San Francisco wholesalers explored funding a coastal shipping route to Astoria, promising a lower freight rate than railroads.[46] Portland leaders did not want Astoria to blossom commercially. Astorian leaders wanted an end to the ability of the

[44] LOC, Chronicling America, *The Morning Astorian*, January 21, 1899.
[45] Ibid., April 20, and May 14, 1899.
[46] Ibid., April 20, 1899. Interested San Francisco merchants were Baker & Hamilton represented by A.C. Rulofson; Holbrook & Merill Stetson represented by W.R. Wheeler, and Miller Sloss and Scott represented by Jospeh Sloss. They had invited Hammond to confer with them at the Palace Hotel on April 14, 1899.

TRULLINGER'S WEST SHORE MILL.

OREGON'S MOST .....
FASHIONABLE RESORT

HOTEL - FLAVEL

J. S. MITCHELL & CO., Lessees.

FLAVEL, ORE.

Steam launch will make trips from Astoria to Flavel every two hours from 7 a. m. to midnight every day during the

ASTORIA - ANNUAL REGATTA

FREE TO HOTEL FLAVEL GUESTS

Hotel Rates—$2 to $3 per day with board. Secure rooms by telephone

Oregon Railroad and Navigation Company to oppress their city's commercial prospects by keeping train traffic expensive.

Others harbored railroad fantasies too. A Mr. Gerlinger and a Dr. Stapleton resumed surveying land for the Columbia River Valley Road. This survey directly impacted the quarantine station. Dr. Hastings learned that they wanted to run the railroad through the station's territory, just a few yards away from any future hospital and the living quarters of the attendants.

This was the commercial context Hastings had to pay attention to. There was always the pressure of growth, growth, and growth without much inquiry into why or for what beyond individual economic reward. Somehow it seemed a given that such commercial passions would withstand any furious diseases that nature might send. And, somehow, Hastings was to assure that such hubris would become true.

Hill Hastings never joined this outlook and politely focused on public health work, rather, how to conduct successful public health work amid such commercial intoxication. Once he showed moderate amounts of social grace to some who mattered in Astoria. In august 1899 he rented, with his own funds, Hotel Flavel and transported party guests to his festivity, renting the *Electric*.[47] This remained the only party he hosted for fellow citizens. His successor would be involved in at least half a dozen more celebrations. Dr. Hastings did not speak openly nor act in opposition to commercial megalomania. So, by September 1899, he became accepted as part of the city's medical establishment.[48] His transition from Seattle to Astoria was unfolding appropriately with quiet, subtle grace. However, there were challenges.

[47] Ibid., August 16, 1899.

[48] Hastings might even have seen Oregon Governor Theodor Greer as he came to Astoria to enjoy Astoria's yearly regatta. Recently Greers first wife had passed away. While attending the regatta Governor Greer met Isabell Trullinger the daughter of the well-known Trullinger family. When he fell in love with her little did he know he was falling in love with the sister of the future engineer of the quarantine station.

HOTEL FLAVEL, FLAVEL, OREGON.

[6]
Smallpox Again In Town and Plague in the News

IN THE LAST WEEK of September, Portland's leadership decided to confront the persistence of smallpox in a more aggressive way. On September 28, Portland's school board met and mandated that school children be vaccinated against smallpox. Otherwise, they could not return to school the next week. By October, Astoria's school board faced the same issue. Would they, too, impose a vaccination mandate for children? Suddenly the rumor emerged that a man called Beecher Sloop had self-quarantined because of plague.[49] Could smallpox and plague exist at the same time in 1899 in Astoria? The answer to this question involved Dr. Hill Hastings.

A nurse invited him to join City Physician Dr. Henderson,[50] Dr. Bishop, and former county health officer Dr. Estes to travel to Beecher Sloop's house. When they found him, he agreed to be examined. Fortunately, the medical team did not find elevated boils under his skin, suggesting bubonic plague but "only" smallpox. For once, seeing a well-developed case of smallpox caused relief in the Northwest.

Back in Astoria, school board members did decide in favor of mandated vaccination of children. The following Saturday was used to give children a shot. However, on Monday, when too few

[49] The committee consisted of City Physician Dr. H.L. Henderson, accompanied by Dr. Hill Hastings, Dr. O.B. Estes, Dr. Bishop, Mr. Flanders, the professional nurse, and Chief of Police Hallock. U.S. Department of Treasury, Public Health Reports, Weekly Reports, Vol. 15, No.10, p. 511. (Hereafter cited as USPHS Weekly Reports).

[50] LOC, *The Morning Astorian*, October 13, 1899. On October 12 Mayor Bergman confirmed Henderson's appointment.

SHIP TRAFFIC IN THE BAY OF KNAPPTON NEXT TO THE EMERGING QUARANTINE STATION.

MAIN OFFICE
AT ASTORIA OREGON.

NERIES LOCATED AT
ASTORIA, OREGON.
EAGLE CLIFF, WASH.
KNAPPTON, WASH.
NORTH SHORE, WASH.

PACKERS OF
EUREKA STAR, EPI
PALM,
BEACON, DESDEMO
AND
OTHER BRANDS O
COLUMBIA RIVER S

CABLE ADDRESS."

Dict. by G.H.G. *Salmon and Commission.*

Astoria, Or. Sept. 5th, 1898.

Dr. D. A. Carmichael,

City,

Dear Sir:-

Referring to our conversation of this morning, concerning t purchase by the Government, for a Quarantine Station, of the r and buildings known as the Knappton Cannery property, located i Pacific County, Washington. We will sell the realty, including shore property and frontage, with buildings and wharves there located, for the sum of $8,000.00 net cash. It is important to that an early decision be arrived at, and this price is made on that condition, as we can not hold the matter open indefinitel because of its possible interference with other propositions w we have in view.

Respectfully yours,

EUREKA & EPICURE PAC

students returned to school, Dr. Henderson offered free vaccination clinics at the building of Fire Brigade Engine No. 2. One hundred twenty-two years later, in 2021, when the COVID-19 Pandemic confronted city officials in Portland and Astoria, this example was forgotten. Eventually, smallpox left Astoria again.

For Dr. Hastings, plague became a permanent priority. In Washington, D. C., U. S. Surgeon General Wyman provided an overview of the status of diseases across the globe as he published every two weeks a segment of the Annual Report of the USPHS. Already on June 27, 1899, he was asked if plague had arrived in Honolulu. Wyman denied it.[51] On the same October day that the Astoria School Board mandated smallpox vaccinations, the public, including Dr. Hastings, learned from Wyman's "Epidemic Notes" that plague had surfaced in Portugal.[52] Interestingly, the local newspaper in St. Helen's, Oregon, had already published the same news on October 6.[53] But, at that time, it was impossible to make a quick drive to St. Helens to have read this news in a paper over breakfast and coffee. No doubt, in 1899, plague was approaching the U. S. from both sides of the world. Until a person ill with plague surfaced in Astoria, Dr. Hastings's target remained luggage, goods, and ballast. He suggested that Washington mandate the opening of cargo and suitcases of all individuals arriving from ports where *Yersinia pestis* was present, regardless of whether a ship needed treatment or quarantine.[54] Dr. Hastings also learned to keep ships with animal transports on his radar screen. The *SS Lennox* was most prominent in Astoria as an animal transporter for the U. S. army. It picked up Oregon mules at the Vancouver, Washington barracks and shipped them to Manila, Philippines.[55]

By the end of October, Portuguese authorities were trying to keep the plague moving west to the Canary Islands. Three weeks

[51] Astoria, Astoria Public Library, *ADB*, June 27, 1899, front page.
[52] USPHS, Weekly Reports, Vol. 14, No. 41, October 13, 1899, USPHS. 1735-1736.
[53] LOC, Chronicling America, St. Helen Oregon Mist, October 6, 1899.
[54] NARA, RG 90, Hastings to Washington, D. C., May 24, 1899.
[55] Astoria Library, *ADB*, June 8, 1899.

LETTER, EUREKA & EPICURE CO. TO DR. CARMICHAEL, SEPTEMBER 5, 1898.

later, it was raising its head in Alexandria, Egypt.[56] Despite the dangerous news in D. C., the transformation of the cannery continued at a snail's pace. Shipping companies wanted it opened soon. The Northern Pacific Steamship Company manager, Mr. Frank Woolsey, asked Dr. Hastings if he could inspect future immigrants at the station once it opened. Usually, it was deputy tax collector Parker who examined individuals, especially those entering within the discrimination of the Chinese Exclusion Act.[57] Hastings forwarded Woolsey's request to Surgeon General Wyman, who passed it on to the commissioner general of immigration.[58]

On September 6, Seattle's U. S. District attorney informed Dr. Hastings and Dr. Wyman that the station's property title was now legal. Still, both men were asked to wait. Dr. Wyman first needed to hold, in his hands, the documents in Washington, D. C.. In mid-October, he reassured Hastings that he expected to receive them very shortly. But the details of what very shortly meant remained undefined. Then, more weeks passed. Construction had to wait without an update.

As troubling as that was, Hastings still did not have permanent control over his means of transportation. Once, Dr. Hastings and Babbidge explored buying the *Electric*. Babbidge mentioned a price of $3,800, and he admitted that the ship needed a new $2,500 boiler. Buying the *Electric* would not be a good deal. Hastings passed on this option.

At least he and his superiors specified what ship they wanted in theory. It should have a shape allowing it to plow through the river in summer and winter, perhaps even during light icy conditions. Other specifics were: seventy-five feet in length fitted with cushioned seats on boards to function as banks. For the engine, they desired a triple expansion or compound engine plus tubular

56 USPHS, November 13, 1900 , p. 4 and "Bubonic plague in Alexandria," *Salem Daily Journal.*

57 Astoria City Library, *ADB*, May 17, 1899 "About the City."

58 NARA, RG 90, Hill Hastings to supervising surgeon general D. C., letter, May 24, 1899; ibid., Wyman to commissioner general of immigration, note, June 3, 1899.

boilers. Comfortably, it should break the surface with a speed of twelve to thirteen knots and be able to venture as far as twenty-five miles from Astoria.[59] An Astorian shipyard was expected to charge $9,000 to $10,000 for such a construction. Again, Hastings failed to initiate negotiations. Now it would be summer 1900, at the earliest, until a federally owned ship could exist that only he could command.

When the first *Electric* contract expired on October 10, 1899, Hastings counseled in favor of a ten-month renewal. In the end, such a contract was signed, and the *Electric*'s rental price became $150 per month.[60]

Hastings always had to deal with purchasing wood, another word for fuel for the *Electric*. Only a guaranteed supply of wood would fire the *Electric's* boilers and carry the medical professionals to inspection. Prices for cords fluctuated. In June, a cord had cost nine dollars and sixty cents; in September, eight dollars; then in October, eleven dollars. Such fluctuations were irritating for Washington bureaucrats who wanted to plan and have everything in just the right place at the beginning of the year. In mid-October, Hastings requested authority to acquire a larger amount of wood for the steamer.

So far, Hastings has purchased wood from the Columbia River sawmill. In November, Washington, D.C. ordered him to end this relationship and switch to Callendar's Knappton Mills instead. Hastings was surprised to learn that the Knappton company refused to enter a contract. The *Electric* did not undertake enough journeys, it was argued, to warrant a long-term contract.[61] It was not the first time Mr. Callendar and his enterprises refused to serve the USPHS, nor would it be the last time.

---

[59] Ibid., Hastings to D.C., letter, September 19, 1899.
[60] Ibid., RG 90, *Electric* files, no date, about October 1899.
[61] Ibid., Hastings to D.C., November 22nd 1899.

[7]
The Context of Hill Hastings's Work Changes

PLAGUE MOVED CLOSER TO Dr. Hastings. On December 9th, in Honolulu, a bookkeeper became ill. Two days later, he was examined by a group of doctors. On December 12th, they declared that Honolulu had one case of plague. The virus found a way to traverse the distance from Asia to Hawaii, which is half of the Pacific Ocean. The other half, the stretch from Hawaii to San Francisco, Astoria, or Seattle, was still unbreeched. But this was not the only advance. *Yersinia pestis* also crossed the Atlantic Ocean.

The USPHS weekly brochure reported one bubonic case in Rio de Janeiro, Brazil, and one in Bahia, Brazil. A few months later, plague was present in Cozumel, Mexico. Dr. Hastings learned that even in northern Europe, officials were preparing for it. In Bremen, Germany, they began to kill rats precautionarily.[62] Plague was possible to track, even slow down, but it was impossible to stop its fourth trip around the globe in 1,000 years. All across the U. S., thirteen USPHS stations, twenty-seven full-time medical officers, seven stewards, and 150 attendants were readying themselves to meet it for the first time. In 1900, that would mean boarding 4,971 ships for inspection. Five hundred ninety-seven of them were disinfected.

Astoria and Oregon leaders could have learned how to prepare from prior incidents in Europe or Asia. What could it mean to be prepared? If one of Astoria's leaders would have traveled to a university library in Eugene, San Francisco, or Seattle and consulted a

[62] Ibid., No. 5, Feb 2, Vol. 15, p. 250.

HONOLULU, CHINATOWN FIRE DURING THE 1900 PLAGUE EPIDEMIC.

book about plague in Venice in 1630, he or she could have learned that already 300 years ago the Venetian government gave special financial help to citizens just like U. S. presidents would do during the 2021 Covid pandemic. Planning could have meant deciding who in Astoria should receive extra payments and under what conditions. The example of Venice also taught that in the words of one eyewitness: "more people were killed by unemployment than by the disease." Any presence of plague would be a dramatic medical event plus a shock to employment and economic activities. In 1630 the Venetian senate contributed income to citizens who had to stay home due to quarantine. Furthermore, just like we discussed a millionaire's tax in 2021, this "pay" to those locked up was financed by a tax from rich Venetians who could afford such a burden. Local banks distributed the funds to the ill and unemployed. Ultimately, the amount spent exceeded the bank's reserves. Politicians rescued it. Already they feared the rage of those impacted most by the disease. Venetian politicians made it a goal to have stable food prices during the outbreak to avoid serious unrest.[63] Little was grown in Astoria, so Hammond and his friends could have asked where a guaranteed food supply would come from during a plague pandemic. However, none of this happened.

John Fox, Astoria's customs officer, sat in his office further down from Dr. Hastings on 661 Commercial Street. He, too, inspected incoming ships, but his focus was a cargo's value and custom rates. From his commercial point of view, the year 1900 promised to earn more custom fees than ever before.

Fox was highly supportive of establishing a direct shipping connection between San Francisco and Portland but also an Astoria to Asia connection. Just as interesting was that British leaders were about to hand U. S. president McKinley the rights to build the Panama Canal. It would take a few years to scratch this deep gap through the narrow isthmus of northern Columbia.

[63] Germany, *Frankfurter Allgemeine Zeitung*, "Pandemie und Helikoptergeld," December 29, 2021, p. 25.

But then, a successful opening would allow wheat fleets to travel faster from England and Germany to Portland, no longer endangered by sailing around the jagged cliffs of South America. The previous year, ships stopping in Astoria and Portland carried ten million bushels of wheat out of the Northwest and into the world. Seven ships sailed to Great Britain in September and nineteen vessels in December 1899.[64] This expanding "grain fleet" grew to one hundred vessels in 1910.[65] Its crews and their health concerned Dr. Hastings.

Colonial wars in Africa, the British Dutch Boer War, reduced available shipping space that European ships, usually returning to Europe via Asia, India, and Africa used and were now changing direction and sailing east. They crossed the Pacific to Astoria in the justified expectation that they might catch a load of wheat and earn a higher income. For example, Hamburg's Rickmer fleet began to show up in Astoria in 1899, trying to take advantage of global fluctuations in shipping space rates.[66]

Custom collector John Fox, too, was aware that, one day soon, plague might appear in Astoria. But no source suggests that he considered seriously that all that trade might come to a sudden halt due to *Yersinia pestis*. Like others in town, he lied to himself, arguing that, at first, plague might only pester the workflow.

But, if it would come to nest in town, this outlook was questionable. Finish sailors would not just keep on throwing their nets into the river's currents. Why should Chinese and Japanese contract workers continue stoically to cut open freshly caught salmon and not desert cannery workspaces? Would they not feel the same fear as Dr. Hastings, Dr. Fulton, or Hammond's secretary residing in the posh Continental Hotel?

---

[64] George Kramer, "Grain, flour and ships: The Wheat Trade in Portland, Oregon," Heritage Associates, Inc. Eugene Oregon, accessed January 3rd, 2022, p. 14.

[65] Ibid., p. 15.

[66] Heinz Burmester, Uwe Jarchow, Walter Kresse, "Grosssegler Rickmer Rickmers: Seine wechselvolle Geschichte, (Hamburg: Ernst Kabel Verlag 1986), 57 ff.

In essence, Dr. Hastings was taken for granted and expected to keep track of these growing numbers of ships and their crews. Somehow, he was expected to vaccinate them and pull the rats out of their ship's hulls. Hastings was never giddy over the growth Fox hoped for. 1900 would be the most challenging year of his career, balancing approaching plague against commercial expansion. It would be thirteen long months as plague tried to gain a foothold on the U. S. West Coast. A comparative challenge—the Spanish Flue—was still nineteen years away. The Covid Pandemic would not paralyze the northwest for another 122 years. Hill Hastings had to master this challenge by the seams of his pants.

Events in Honolulu were hints of what he might experience. Officials focused on containing plague by no longer allowing crew members to leave their vessels for tours of the port district. Second, authorities imposed a ten-day quarantine over the city. Trade across the Pacific was completely interrupted for the first time in memory. And yet numbers of infected citizens did not drop. To the contrary, they grew. Christmas 1899, nine additional sick individuals were counted.[67] Then Honolulu's port operators changed their minds and reopened it. The USPHS had no choice but to work within this commercial coming and going.

Bureaucrats in Washington, D. C. did not hurry to help Hastings with extra measures. They announced they would purchase one steam chamber for the station, a second apparatus that distributed formaldehyde, and a third machine to mix sulfur with oxygen. In addition, they purchased pipes and hoses to be assembled so that a sulfur air mix could be blown into a ship's hull. After this chemical attack on invisible critters, a fan and an exhaust system would blow the fumes back out onto the shorelines of Washington state.[68]

Shelf-ready fumigation machinery and disinfection technology did not exist. The station's two Hugh Steam Disinfecting Chambers were yet to be manufactured in Philadelphia. Even if Hastings held

---

[67] NLM, Kinyoun Papers, USPHS, James K. Ikeda, Vol. 25, March 1, 1885; A brief history of Plague in Hawaii, p.1.

[68] Astoria, CCHS, Folder: Trullinger, Letter, Trullinger, March 2nd , 1900.

WHEAT FIELD, UMATILLA COUNTY, 1936.

KENSINGTON ENGINE WORKS CO.

"Kinyoun-Francis" Disinfecting Machinery

Beach and East Berks Streets

PHILADELPHIA, PA.

PRODUCTS. We manufacture the "KINYOUN-FRANCIS" DISINFECTING, STERILIZING, and FUMIGATING APPARATUS for Hospitals, Asylums, Boards of Health, and Quarantine Stations. JACKETED STEAM CHAMBERS, SULPHUR DIOXIDE FURNACES, PORTABLE and STATIONARY FORMALDEHYDE GENERATORS.

"KINYOUN-FRANCIS" DISINFECTING CHAMBER ERECTED FOR OPERATION
Showing the Car and Track Supports and Formaldehyde Apparatus

DESCRIPTION. The wall separating the infected end from the disinfected end is placed in line with either saddle; the saddle is then built in the wall. It is preferable to have the

the building's title in his hand free and clear in 1899, it would be months before the technology would arrive that could vanquish *Yersinia pestis*. For at least six months, Hastings's emergency setup on Astoria's dock would have to do.

Dr. Hastings's steps remained measured and rational in the midst of growing fear in the bay. On January 9, 1900, fumigation was made mandatory for all ships arriving from Honolulu. A captain showing only a certificate of health was no longer enough. Ten days later, on January 19, the USPHS ordered all Pacific stations to make the search for plague a sustained priority. Seven days later, a newly published mandate demanded the fumigation of luggage arriving on ships from Honolulu.[69] U. S. Surgeon General Wyman dispatched additional health professionals. From San Francisco, Ichitaro Katsuki was sent to Honolulu to observe Hawaiian health officers' actions and collaborate in their pathological studies.[70] Three additional officers were sent to Port Townsend, Washington; one to Eureka, California, and one to San Diego, California. But Dr. Hastings in Astoria received no additional helper even though the U. S. government promised to pour an additional $300,000 into the fight to keep plague out of our coasts.[71] Once again, the Columbia River region was ignored.

Even during the threat of plague approaching, Hastings had to make do with only $640 per month.[72] His first published budget covered March to June 1900. Hastings's salary was the largest line item listed at $181.90. In addition, he paid three individuals. They were *Electric's* captain Babbidge and attendant Riles A. Hendriff, each earning ninety dollars. And, deckhand Edward Muddeman received fifty dollars. Whether a secretary worked for Hastings at

69 USPHS, Weekly Report, Vol. 15, No.4. January 26, p. 147-203.

70 Guenter B. Riese, *Plague, Fear and Politics In San Francisco's Chinatown,...* (Baltimore: John Hopkins Press, 2012).

71 USPHS, Weekly Report, Vol.15, No.3, January 19, 1900, p. 97-98.Ibid., No. 4., January 26, p. 147-203.

72 NARA, RG 90, Hill Hastings, to Supervising Surgeon General, Washington, D.C. , March 12, 1900. The exact budget amounts were: March $647,50; April $640,50; May $645,80;June $641,50, for a total of $2576,20.

SUCH A KINYOUN-FRANCIS DISINFECTING MACHINE WAS OPERATED INSIDE THE STATION.

Estimate of Expenses for month of June
at
Columbia River Quarantine Station

	$	
Pay, Assistant Surgeon Hastings	131	90
Pay, Employees, crew of Boarding Steamer	230	
Commutation for Quarters, Asst Surg Hastings	30	
Rent of Steamer "Electric", as Boarding Steamer	150	
Rent of dock	5	
Rent of office, heat and lights	10	
Fuel for Steamer	15	
Supplies	20	
Repairs to broken guard on steamer	25	
Emergency Expenses, as disinfecting labor &c	25	
Total	$641	90

this time remains to be discovered. On the station's payroll, he or she was not mentioned.

Hastings received thirty dollars for monthly rent. His monthly amount of petty cash was only twenty-five dollars. Everything else was first ordered and approved in Washington, D.C. The doctor spent what Washington told him to first.

Around Astoria, animals and people carried on as usual. In January, salmon saw no reason not to swim toward the Columbia's mouth. Also, in 1900, nature would not interrupt this yearly migration because of the advance of disease. In Finland, 3,000 men enjoyed their last eight weeks at home before embarking on their yearly Atlantic crossing to Astoria. There, at the end of April, the fishing season would begin.[73] Opposite the globe of Finland, in China and Japan, and among Chinese American and Japanese American communities, people readied themselves to arrive in Astoria in late April. They would staff the world's largest cluster of industrial salmon processing plants. Finns would sail and catch fish, and Chinese, Japanese, Chinese Americans, and Japanese Americans would can the fish. Everybody in town knew of this ethnic division of labor and maintained it. All these flows of fish and men alike passed near Dr. Hastings's office. Somehow, he was expected to deal with all of them and keep people disease free. Plus, he was not to complain as business people let more ships into the river. Hastings was expected to perform a miracle and prevent what was occurring in Honolulu, Rio de Janeiro, Egypt, and Kanton.

On Thursday, January 4th, 1900, it was defined what this would mean for Astoria. That day Hastings announced that the plague in Honolulu "will cause the quarantine regulations at this port to be particularly severe." Then, Astoria journalists exaggerated what Dr. Hastings had just said. A choir of select newspaper writers whistled in the dark, swearing emphatically, "Hill Hastings has all

[73] For three more years their boats would cross the bay with wind power without making much noise. After 1903, outboard combustion engines were introduced and fishing season became a noisy affair.

ONE OF THE STATION'S EARLIEST MONTHLY BUDGETS.

preparations ready to see that it does not enter this port."[74] Clearly, this was not just an exaggeration but hubris against nature.

Four days later seven new cases of plague were announced in Honolulu.[75] Authorities in the Hawaiian capital were now burning quarters belonging to individuals suspected to be close to plague. Would fire burnings take place in Astoria too?

The public tone in Astoria made a noticeable shift. Representatives of shipping companies expressed sudden interest in what the government was doing to establish a thoroughly equipped station at Astoria. Prior champions of free enterprise now called for the federal government to assure that the yearly rhythms of industrial, maritime life would not be disturbed. Even though a few weeks ago, they had enjoyed Hill Hastings pretending that, for sure, he would be able to keep the disease out of the bay, observers now showed a greater sense of reality. Businessmen had to accept that "it will require considerable time to complete the quarantine plant ready for service as much of machinery had to be manufactured." In public, Hastings kept a stiff upper lip. Again, he assured that in the meantime, he could take care of ships coming from foreign ports.[76] He helped deflect justified fear when he suggested that "a properly equipped station is only necessary when a vessel has on board passengers whose clothing and baggage must be disinfected." Such words made light of a very problematic situation.

Even in such a stressful situation, city leaders remained stingy. They could have designated a pest house in Astoria. Instead, they decided to wait for Hastings's station to open. Then, they too, intended to use the USPHS station as the city's pest house.[77]

Hastings had no choice other than striking a balance between health and commerce. On January 22, 1900, he asked manager Wolsey of the Northern Pacific steamship line to set aside articles for disinfection from ships coming from Honolulu. It was announced that all of them probably will be thoroughly fumigated

[74] Astoria, Astoria Public Library, *ADB*, January 4th, 1900, "About the City."
[75] Ibid., January 9, 1900, "About the City."
[76] Ibid., January 20, 1900, "About the City."
[77] Ibid., February 28, 1900, "About the City."

Abstract of Title

—TO—

A portion of Lot 3, Section

17, Twp. 9, North of Range 9 W.

as shown by the various records of the County

of Pacific, State of Washington.

MADE AT THE REQUEST OF

Eureka & Epicure Packing Co.

this 13 *day of* Jan. 1890

A. P. LEONARD,

ABSTRACTER,

SOUTH BEND, - - WASHINGTON.

Reproduced at the National Archives at Seattle

whether or not there is any sickness on board. Special care will be taken to kill all rats as the experience of the service has shown that these animals are dangerous agents for spreading the infection.[78]

Also, Hastings moved further away from town interactions with incoming ships. For example, when the *Marionneth* arrived, she was fumigated inside the bay but was no longer next to Astoria's wharf.[79]

Suddenly, on January 22nd, joyful news about the station interrupted the watchful waiting around the bay. U.S. Surgeon General Wyman cabled from Washington, D.C. that the cannery's title arrived and that former owner Hume received his $8,000 payment. Suddenly, Hastings had the right to pry open the cannery's doors and begin reconstruction.

When Hastings studied updates about the global journey of plague, he saw contradictions. On the eastern side of the Americas, plague was spreading southward. On the 24th of January, the newspaper reported that Argentina was now an American capital with plague present.[80] From Honolulu, opposite news arrived. There, an unlikely victory over the disease was promised. Officer Townsend of the *Nanyo Maru* reported that the situation was improving in Honolulu, and "a feeling of security was prevailing in the city."[81] On February 9th, newspapers insisted that "the disease was substantially under control—the greatest danger was past."[82] However, the reality was far more complicated. In Hawaii, public health work was going terribly wrong. On January 20th, "fire cleansing" resumed. Unexpectedly, winds picked up the flames this time, and the "controlled burn" exploded into an uncontrollable inferno that began to eat 3,800 acres. For seventeen days, it devoured 4,000 houses. February 6th was the soonest the flames could be extinguished.

78 Ibid., January 24, 1900, "About the City."
79 Ibid., January 26, 1900, "maritime news".
80 Ibid., January 20, 1900, "About the City."
81 Ibid., January 31, 1900, "About the City."
82 Ibid., February 9, 1900."About the City."

ABSTRACT OF TITLE OF STATION.

[8]
A First Fortunate Scare: Nature Waves A Medical Fencepole

IF IN THOSE MONTHS, gods were looking out for Astoria, they showed mercy. Nature administered a gentle push, nudging city leaders to consider how to implement better structures to deal with a public health crisis. One new case of smallpox appeared. Mr. Townsend, a visitor, and his wife, most likely from Baker City, brought smallpox to Astoria while taking up residence in the Central Hotel. Since leaders just voted not to open a city pest house, no facility existed where Mr. and Mrs. Townsend could be isolated.

City doctors, not Hill Hastings, handled the resulting scare. They decided to turn one floor of the Central Hotel into a quarantine floor. One suite of rooms was confiscated, a guard and a nurse were stationed in front of it, and Mr. Townsend was kept inside.[83] Mrs. Townsend was vaccinated. After that, Doctor Henderson fumigated the Central Hotel's ground, first, and second floors.[84]

Nature's nudge worked. City doctor Henderson voiced louder public noise demanding more attention from Astoria's leadership. First, he complained that nature, scope, and pay of his position remained poorly defined. To him, his appointment seemed even questionable. This time Astoria's elite listened better. At the end

[83] His name was R.T. Townsend.
[84] Astoria, Astoria Public Library, *ADB*, February 9 and 10, 1900, "About the City."

Dr. H. L.
HENDERSON

of the week, the city council met, officially appointed Henderson, and granted him a monthly payment of fifty dollars. In addition, they instituted new public health measures that were not specific to smallpox or plague. But they mattered. For example, for the first time, the city required the inspection of all meat for sale. Second, an official standard was established that defined how a sewage pipe should be connected to a house.

DR. HENDERSON, NEWSPAPER PHOTOGRAPH AND CARICATURE.

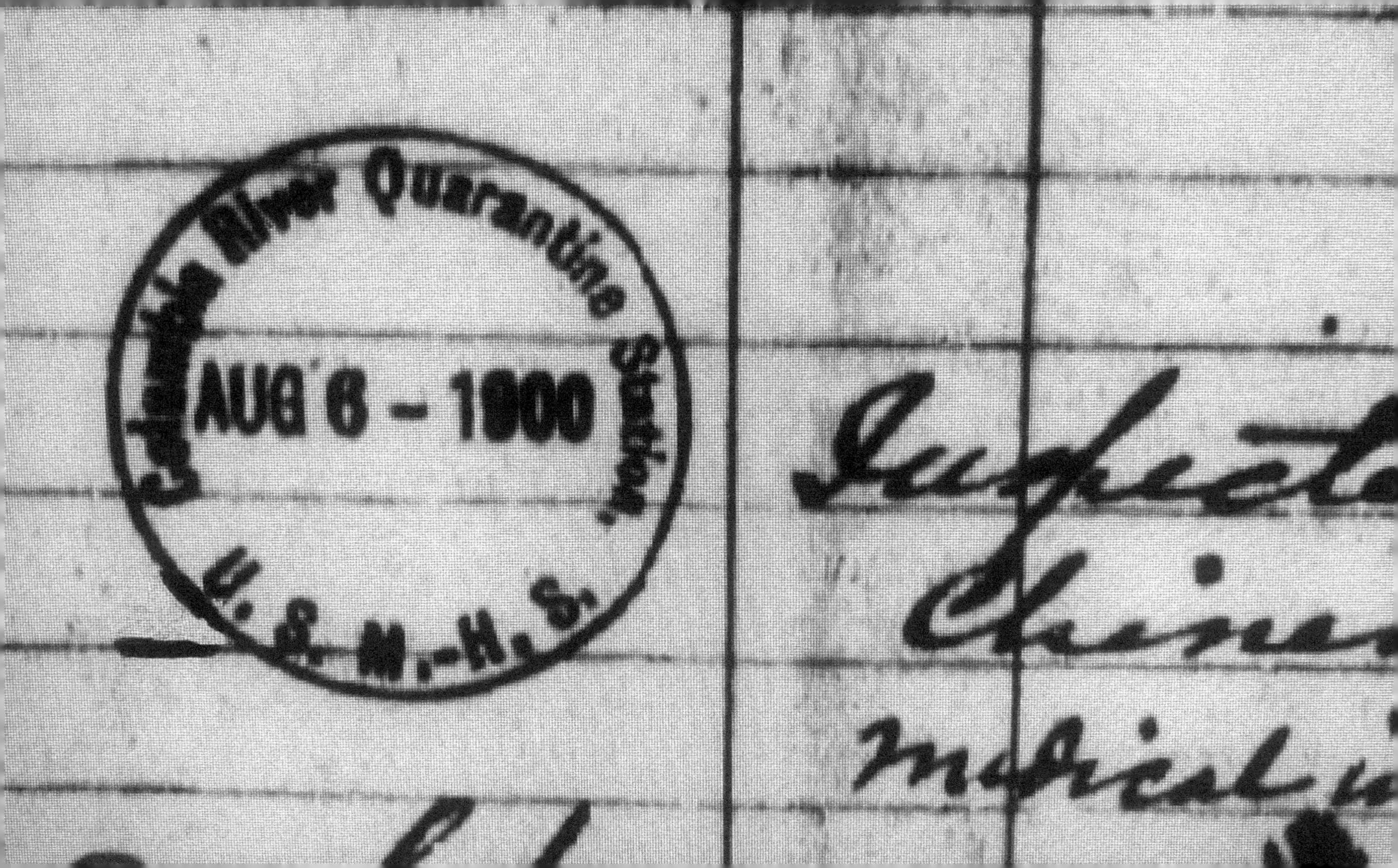
River Quarantine Station,
AUG 6 - 1900
U. S. M.-H. S.

[9]

From Disregard to First Action

HENDERSON FELT EMBOLDENED, STRONG enough to move from talking about measures to instituting some. On February 19th, he inspected the entire city, looking for serious diseases, and found none. More importantly, he joined Astoria's medical leaders and co-published a shared outlook toward the approaching plague. Nine doctors signed it: Oregonian health officer Dr. Fulton, city physician H. L. Henderson, M. D. August C. Kinney and his brother Alfred Kinney, U. S. army doctor Geo A. Skinner, Johan S. Bisley, Dr. J Tuttle, Dr. O. B. Estes, and the station's Dr. Hill Hastings.[85] These were nine key voices that mattered in town. Their statement warned Astorians and citizens of Clatsop County about plague possibly entering the town. At least Astoria's medical community began to take seriously the prospect that it might enter the bay soon.

This statement marked the beginning of phase two where events in Astoria began to relate more and more to what truly happened in San Francisco and Honolulu. U. S. cities where the disease had already surfaced. It might be called the pre-plague stage. Today, in hindsight, we know that luck kept the pre-plague stage from becoming the next stage: the presence of plague in the city.[86]

Between February and May 3, three phases can be distinguished. From February to March 8th, all key medical personnel

[85] LOC, Chronicling America, *The Morning Astoria*, February 27, 1900, image 3.

[86] Of course the acts of the USPHS contributed significantly to reenforce this luck.

A FIRST STAMP PRINTING THE QUARANTINE STATION'S NAME.

in town spoke in unison during this first phase. All approached the plague through the eyes of natural science, regardless of whether they were self-employed, served the State of Oregon, or were paid by the government in Washington, D. C.

The second phase, from March 8th to May 21st, was marked by the words and advice of one man—Dr. Alfred C. Kinney. He put forth a vision that included insights from public health measures learned by Imperial Japan. To him, the Asian exclusion laws and their anti-Chinese and anti-Japanese sentiments mattered less. His advocacy remained a constant and admirable reminder that the disease was something different than a "Chinese virus."

The third phase, beginning May 21st, was marked by the split of Dr. Fulton and at least one of his brothers away from a previous scientific outlook and a move to see the disease as an ethnic—"racial" event. In addition, regional doctors attempted to put Oregon law ahead of federal law.

A look at phase one reveals that from January to March 8, 1900, doctors correctly identified a bacillus and rodents as agents that spread the disease. The flea-carrying *Yersinia pestis* would bite the Chinese crew member just as it happily pricked the German sailor. The *Morning Astorian* praised the doctor's February statement issued during this time as "timely and [it] should be headed." Also noteworthy is that unlike in San Francisco, Astoria's press did not break away from commercial interests and backed the doctors' public stance. All stakeholders praised a determined deadly pursuit of rats for preventing the disease from gaining a foothold. All rats should be poisoned living near and in people's homes. What to do with rats found on incoming foreign ships was still left up to the USPHS.

Commercial salmon fishing circles owning the *Morning Astorian* proclaimed overly optimistic incantations during these weeks. Editors commented with respect:

Danger was not immanent, but it is well known that the government's Marine Hospital Service is active and vigilant and well prepared. With the precaution and the intelligent cooperation of local physicians such as professing in Astoria [...] the danger of plague can at least be reduced to a minimum even if its outbreak cannot be altogether prevented.[87]

Days later, Dr. Hastings began transforming the cannery into a quarantine station. On February 28th, he took the *Electric* across the bay to measure the depth of the channel in front of the building. His gage announced twenty-three feet at low tide and thirty-six feet at high tide. This depth was enough to proclaim the shipping channel viable for incoming and outgoing ocean vessels at any time.[88]

Also, Hastings began staffing open positions. In 1900, not many individuals lived in Pacific County, WA, or Clatsop County, OR, with a good work record and solid work experience operating machinery distributing toxic chemicals. As a doctor, he was not expected to throw chemicals into furnaces or to lay pipe into a ship's hull. That would be the task of a station engineer. This technician was to keep the technical apparatus in excellent running order so that, at any time, it could be used.

A certain smile on our faces is appropriate when we learn that U.S. Customs Collector John Fox led this search committee, too. Should we be surprised to realize that Fox's daughter was married to Thaddeus Trullinger, the man who would apply for the position? Furthermore, it could not hurt to ponder that Thaddeus Trullinger was the brother of the soon-to-be second wife of Oregon's governor Greer. The USPHS station was becoming part of local, regional, and even national social networks.

Nevertheless, in public, a respectful process was presented. On March 1, 1900, Samuel Gordon, cashier of Astoria's First National

[87] LOC, Chronicling America, *The Astoria Morning Astorian*, Feb, 27, 1000, image 2.

[88] Astoria, Astoria Public Library, *ADB*, February 28, 1900, "About the City."

Bank, wrote a letter recommending Thaddeus Trullinger. A second letter, written by Mr. Hill, an employee of the Trullinger family's West Shore Mills Company, assured the USPHS that Thaddeus Trullinger was "a competent man handling steam engines and electrical machinery." His superior at the mill expressed how sorry the mill was to see Trullinger leave after ten years of employment.[89] With these two letters in hand, Thaddeus Trullinger applied to Dr. Hastings on March 2nd, 1900.[90] There could not have been any doubt about the outcome of this search.

[89] Astoria, Clatsop County Historical Society, Folder: Trullinger , letter, Hill, West Shore Mill Company, March 2nd, 1900.
[90] The meeting took place April 31st, 1900.

[10]
When Nature is a Reaper and not a Mother

SUDDENLY, NATURE DISRUPTED DR. Hastings's forward movement again. In San Francisco, the owner of a lumber yard had visited a doctor stating that he had been strangely ill for more than a week. A day later, he died. The autopsy of his body by the San Francisco police surgeon and the city health commissioner diagnosed the presence of swollen lymph nodes. Without a doubt, in front of them was the cadaver of a human being destroyed by plague. No doubt, plague made the final journey from Honolulu to the U. S. West Coast by March 1900.

In San Francisco, doctors took cultures from the corps and sent a sample to the USPHS laboratory on Angel Island. Station director Dr. Kinyoun injected specimens into two guinea pigs, one rat, and a small monkey. The monkey died within eighty-two hours.[91] Right away from Washington, D. C. Surgeon General Wyman attempted to persuade city officials to inoculate all inhabitants of Chinatown with Hoffkine's Prophylactic. This anti-cholera vaccine was the standard treatment in China and India at that time. Moreover, the USPHS imposed a partial quarantine over Chinatown but not the rest of San Francisco, lasting from March 6th to March 9th.[92] Then, twenty-five doctors, fifty policemen, and 120 inspectors began

[91] Echenberg, Myron. *Plague Ports: The Global Urban Impact of Bubonic Plague, 1894-1901*. NYU Press, 2007. p. 116, 117.
[92] NLM, Joseph Kinyoun Papers, "to my dear Aunt and Uncle, June 29, 1901." PDF, accessed January 2nd, 2022.

inspecting of this part of town.[93] But such a clean-up of a city was not the same as a systematic health campaign that included quarantine. Owners of residences chose avoidance, fearing that eventually, in San Francisco, residences would be burned down as had been in Honolulu. In this chaos, Randolph Hearst's newspapers played a devastating role in spreading news in the most dramatic terms so that justified fears were whipped toward hysteria.[94] On March 7th, the death in San Francisco was announced to the public. Traffic in and out of Chinatown remained blocked. Local doctors attempted to check if anybody was infected. The *Astoria Daily Budget* announced it on its front page: "Bubonic Plague! One case discovered in San Francisco!"

[93] Echenberg, *Plague Ports*, (2007) p. 118; Astoria Public Library, *ADB*, March 12, 1900, "About the City."
[94] Echenberg, *Plague Ports*, (2007) p. 118.

[10A]
Projecting a Unified Voice and Vision in Astoria

One day before, in Astoria, a debate about the possibility of plague resumed. In city council, for the third or fourth time, politicians were urged to order precautionary killings of rats.[95] At least a price was suggested for the tiny head of an Astoria rodent: two cents. Dr. Kinney chimed in, adding that the reward for a rat was two cents in Japan. Furthermore, he offered the following scenario:

" one or two infected persons might be isolated and thus prevent spread or contagion from actual contact, but the myriads of rats which are most susceptible to the disease would soon spread it beyond control."[96] He said: "the plague was a grave danger and most likely will be introduced in Astoria and San Francisco; it would be almost a miracle if it does not gain a foothold."

Also, listeners learned that in Manila, Philippines, the U.S. government was paying for rats.

[95] Astoria, Public Library, *ADB*, March 6, 1900, "About the City."
[96] *ADB*, March 6, 1900, "About the City."

[10B]
An Individual Stands Out — Alfred Kinney —

IN THE SECOND WEEK of March, the second phase began. What distinguished it was the voice and suggestions of local doctor Alfred E. Kinney. Nancy Hoffman introduced Alfred E. Kinney's achievements and significance already in 2010. He was president of the Oregon State Medical society, helped found Portland's St. Vincent Hospital, and served as Astoria's mayor and port commissioner.[97] Now, he became the wisest local medical voice.

Kinney demanded that Astorian leaders learn from experiences in Asia while the general public oppressed Asian Americans in San Francisco. He firmly reminded everybody that "the Japanese were leading the world in precautionary measures against plague." That meant depriving *Yersinia pestis* of its means of transportation from town to town by paying a financial reward for catching and killing rats.

Dr. Kinney also showed a practical side, reminding politicians of the impact that any appearance of plague would have on Astoria's city budget. So far, Honolulu had spent $100,000.00. Plus, the city had to pay for blocks lost to fire. Did the city have such funds in case Honolulu's events would repeat in Astoria?[98]

---

[97] Karen Kirtley, *Astorian's: Eccentric and Extraordinary*, (Salem, Oregon: Eastern Oregon Publishing Company) 2010; p. 112.

[98] Astoria, Astoria Public Library, *ADB*, March 6, 1900, "About the City."

DR. ALFRED KINNEY.

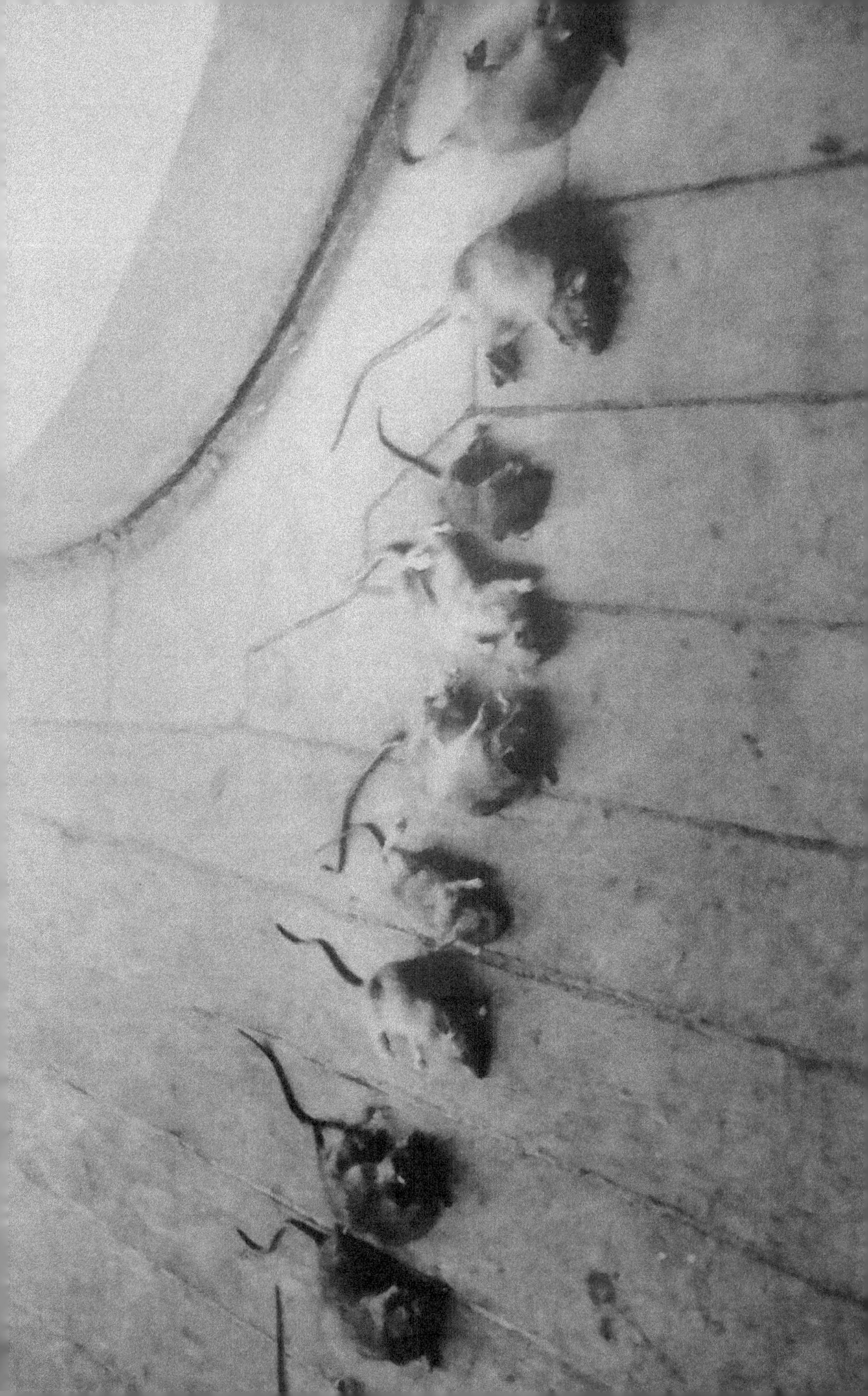

He insisted that focusing on nature as a culprit for the disease was far better than focusing on a person's ethnicity. Kinney's attempt to keep science in the middle of the debate needs to be remembered. Some of the city's leading doctors would throw restraint overboard a few weeks later, assigning blame to people's ethnic origin, forgetting that fleas, bacteria, and the virus were the true culprits.

In theory, Astoria's politicians accepted Dr. Kinney's suggestions. But in practice, they did not hurry to replace debate with acts. The day before plague was confirmed in San Francisco, the city council only moved the issue to a sub-commission for further discussion. More talk, more deliberation, but still no action.

Only the news the next day from San Francisco ended this slow pace. At least Dr. Henderson became more active. Now, he wanted the city council to pass an ordinance that would give him the right

> *"to enforce the purification and disinfection of all filthy premises and possible sources of contamination and pollution that could become a source of menace to the public health in case of the city becoming infected."*[99]

On the same day, Astoria's maritime community heard the rumor that the Japanese ship *Nanu Maru* was stopped further north at Diamond Point. Allegedly, there too, one case of plague had emerged. However, the rumor could not be confirmed.

Debate among Astorian leaders now became more public. On March 10th, Astorian doctor J. E. Bishop demanded in a public letter "to clean up Swilltown." There, all ethnicities and mostly lower social groups celebrated. Nevertheless, when plague would come, it would creep past the tidal flats. The upper crust of society on Franklin Street would be infected just as would the workers of Union Town.

---

[99] Ibid., March 8, 1900, "About the City."

HERE MICE AND RATS ARE PRESENTED THAT WERE CAUGHT ON A SHIP.

Astorian journalists added concerns about the self-defeating tension of being honest about a pandemic and wanting to close a city versus the need to keep it open to earn income. One journalist warned readers that money and commerce might destroy wise practice. He wrote, "it has been a habit of cities to keep any outbreak quiet as they think it hurts their business."[100] Astorian leaders could now compare events in San Francisco, where the plague had just emerged, to those in Honolulu, where the first wave of infection seemed to have passed.[101]

[100] LOC, Chronicling America, The Morning Astorian, March 14, 1900, image 3.

[101] Astoria, Astoria Public Library, *ADB*, "About the City." March 13, 1900.

[10c] The Rotten Ethnic Blame Game

UNDER SUCH PRESSURE, ETHNICITY began to play a greater role in Astorian thinking. Dr. Henderson toured Chinatown "for the purpose of acquainting himself with the locality."[102] Thereafter, he toured the rest of the city, looking for stagnant pools of water.[103] In 1900, such pools of water remained along the entire city waterfront, occasionally refilling during a particularly high tide. Tidal flats had nothing to do with the lifestyle that Chinese Americans had created in Astoria. Tidal flats existed along the entire waterfront.[104]

News from San Francisco remained disheartening. There, wishful thinking and racist commercial priorities were moving to the forefront. Following the one case from early March, no more plague was diagnosed for forty-five days. San Francisco's board of health wanted this to be read as plague disappearing. Mayor Phelan wrote a letter to fifty U.S. mayors saying that no new case in San Francisco was present. Astorians could read this news on the front page.[105] With the exception of USPHS doctors, San Francisco's politicians and citizens increasingly used "plague" as a political football. The terrible disease became a playing card in political struggles between Republicans and Democrats, state versus federal government, and ethnicities versus ethnicities. Also,

102 LOC, Chronicling America, *The Morning Astorian*, March 10, 1900, M.D. Bishop J.E. Letter.

103 Astoria, Astoria Public Library, *ADB*, March 14, 1900, "About the City."

104 Ibid., March 15, 1900, "About the City." USPHS Weekly Reports, Vol. 15, No.14, March 22, 1900, Hill Hastings to Wyman, "Precautions against plague in Astoria Oregon," 769.

105 Astoria, Astoria Public Library, *ADB*, March 27, 1900, "About the City."

urban developers saw the disease and the resulting confusion as just the right pretext to claw control over Chinatown's real estate. They wanted to tear it down only to build new buildings where average Chinese Americans could not afford to live. In San Francisco, greed and the plague entered an unholy alliance.

Also, San Francisco's general public tied the disease to individuals of Chinese background. Obviously, Chinese American individuals resented unjustified ethnic stereotyping and fought back. Unlike in other U. S. cities, the Chinese American community of San Francisco was well organized and marshaled effective political representation. Central to this effort were the six large Chinese companies. They received additional foreign support from the Chinese Consul General of San Francisco. The plague raging in Portugal, Egypt, and Brazil played no role in the minds of any involved party. Would such selective reasoning repeat in Oregon?

In Astoria, a third phase began. The medical community in the town split into two camps. One would continue to follow the path of science. Here, doctors Kinney, Henderson, and Hastings stood out. A second one, close to Dr. Fulton, moved toward what was happening in San Francisco and linked plague with ethnicity.

Dr. Fulton had already argued to prohibit ships and railroad companies from transporting Chinese and Chinese American individuals to Astoria. They should be prohibited from leaving a train or a ship unless they could produce a certificate from an Astoria doctor certifying their health, he demanded. Dr. Fulton also asked Governor Greer to keep Chinese American people out of the state.[106]

Dr. Hill Hastings, too, wrestled with how to proceed. Since plague would most likely come into Astoria from Honolulu or San Francisco, he asked the Surgeon General on March 3rd if ships arriving from those cities should be quarantined.[107] But Surgeon General Wyman answered, "no." Then, the *State of California*

[106] Ibid.,March 16, 1900, "About the City."
[107] Here he referred to the *SS Columbia*.

arrived on Friday, March 16th, 1900. Again, Dr. Hastings asked the U.S. surgeon general for principled direction. Further north in Victoria, B.C., any ship from San Francisco had to enter quarantine. Dr. Hastings was waiting to do things by the book but was looking at a blank page.

The U.S. government gave no support for such a principled future stance. And so, Dr. Hastings suggested letting the "*State of California*" continue on her journey without imposing quarantine.[108] However, Dr. A. J. Fulton thought otherwise and put an ethnic spin on the situation. He informed the OR&N railroad that "any Chinaman" arriving on one of their boats would be prohibited to disembark unless he could show a health certificate "from a reliable citizen" of Astoria. Second, he wrote a letter to Governor Greer asking that he should keep the plague from landing in Astoria. The governor's reply is not known. Dr. Fulton's brother in Salem, Oregon, asked Governor Greer to station supervisors at the California/Oregon border railway stations. They should watch for Californians crossing into Oregon. Suddenly, no Chinese person in Astoria could disembark until Fulton made a final examination and fumigated his luggage.[109] Dr. Fulton insisted that the "*State of California*" had to anchor offshore from Astoria. Then, he investigated the luggage of a Chinese passenger.[110] He mandated the he and his luggage be fumigated.[111]

Astoria's doctors insisting on science also scored a victory. On March 19th, at a city council meeting, Dr. Kinney spoke again about events in Tokyo as lessons for Astoria. He explained that there 100,000 rats were caught within 30 days. A bounty for rats in Astoria would deliver 1,000 rats, he predicted. Then "there would be no danger of an epidemic."[112] This time the politicians not only agreed but also acted. Dr. Hastings informed Surgeon

---

[108] LOC, Chronicling America, *The Morning Astorian*, March 16, 1900. USPHS Weekly Report, Vol. 15, No. 6, Feb. 9, Jas B. Eagleson, p. 267-317.
[109] Astoria Public Library, *ADB*, March 16, 1900, "About the City."
[110] LOC, Chronicling America, "*The Morning Astorian*," March 17, 1900.
[111] Astoria, Astoria Public Library, *ADB*, March 16, 1900, "About the City."
[112] Ibid., *ADB*, March 20, 1900, "About the City."

THE *SS STATE OF CALIFORNIA.*

Prof. Dr. S. Kitasato
S. Yeghi
SHIMBASHI
TOKYO JAPAN.

General Wyman that city leaders agreed to pay a bounty for a rat for thirty days.[113]

Astoria's police chief Hallock scheduled the hour from 6–7 p.m. on March 21st as the time to drop off rats that would be caught. When this hour came, not a single person appeared with a rodent in a bag. Zero were dropped off on day one. The *Astoria Daily Budget* kidded that Astorian rats, too, might be reading the newspaper and had gone into hiding.[114] Once more, Dr. Bishop wrote a public letter arguing that city officials and house owners should handle the rat-catching program. He complained that the killing of rats seemed to be left "to boys or "Chinamen" eager to make money. "As far as he was concerned, the city should spend one time $500 so that a professional exterminator could do the job and render the city proof from infection."

Regular citizens voiced their very own distinct worries. It would be them or their family members performing dangerous plague prevention work. Overnight, plague and average citzens were linked in a most dangerous way. They asked if a rat should be dropped off dead, alive, or in a trap. One person suggested bringing along a dog so that he could bite to death a living rat. Citizens hoped that police chief Hallock would somehow solve this conundrum. But again, no rats were dropped off on March 22nd or 23rd. New rumors suggested that "the boys of town were hoarding animal cadavers." Finally, on March 24th, the police chief reported the arrival of the first two rats. That catch broke the ice. March 25th and 26th registered fifteen rats, bringing the new tally to seventeen rodents. Still, new questions were raised. Parents realized that an infected rat might bite their child in the process of catching it. Increasingly, they were squeamish about the entire process.[115]

---

113 USPHS, Weekly Reports, Vol. 15, No.14, March 22, 1900, Hill Hastings to Wyman, "Precautions against plague in Astoria Oregon," 769.

114 Astoria, Astoria Public Library, *ADB*, March 15, 1900, "About the City." March 15, 1900.

115 Ibid., March 22, 23, 24, 1900, "About the City."

Others focused on staying positive. From the shipping community came praise for Dr. Hastings. At least one captain found his efforts reassuring. Captain Perry of the U. S. Bark *Arago* reported that the USPHS doctor was "doing very thorough work...he was one of the most thorough...he was performing his duties perfectly..."[116] Indeed, when March ended, Dr. Fulton and Dr. Hastings could feel lucky. From January to March 27th, ships journeyed into the bay, and each was certified in good sanitary conditions.[117] Astoria remained plague free.

News from the other side of the Pacific reminded everyone to remain vigilant. They were not any more encouraging. From Manila, new cases of plague were reported. In Sydney, Australia, one hundred suffered from it.[118]

Suddenly Hastings received news that offered a silver lining. He was informed that, in Philadelphia, the Kensington Engine Works had manufactured the fumigation machines he had ordered. Even better, the machines began to make their way to Astoria. Within a few months at the Columbia River, they could crush or steam pathogens out of existence. They could not arrive early enough. One other source reported that Dr. Hastings received a limited amount of serum in case a person with plague might surface in Astoria.[119]

In Washington, D. C. bureaucracy chugged along as if no urgency existed. Still, on April 4th, 1900, Hastings could not report any reaction from Washington, D. C. to the construction proposals he submitted. He still did not know when to open bids for items needed to run the station.[120] This was the situation when the first salmon harvest season of 1900 opened.

---

116 Ibid., March 22, 1900, "About the City." On March 20 Wyman had amended quarantine rules.
117 Eight ships were expected for April; two to arrive in May.
118 Astoria Public Library, *ADB*, April 21,1900, "About the City." Suddenly on April 21 it was announced that plague in Manila had been repressed.
119 Ibid., April 10, 1900, "About the City."
120 Ibid., April 4th, 1900,"About the City."

[11]
Burdening a Station's Doctor with Expectations of Local Business Profit

THIS SPRING, AGAIN, A myriad number of salmons kept rushing toward the Columbia River, hoping to reach their birthplaces. Nature was sending far more fish to Astoria than it sent fleas. Finnish sailors, by now, were close to Astoria, and Japanese laborers were approaching the west coast of the U. S., trying to take advantage of the Chinese exclusion laws. More than a thousand were approaching San Francisco, eager to venture on to Astoria and Seattle to work in the scheduled harvest. Nobody ever asked aloud how and if the 1900 salmon harvest would unfold if one flea on a rat would reach Astoria and establish plague among cannery workers. Dr. Hastings most certainly was aware that closing the mouth of the river for any reason was extremely unlikely and stopping the harvest was impossible. Regardless of the experience in Honolulu and San Francisco, most people in Astoria only wanted to increase the commercial use of the river. And, of course, it was Dr. Hastings who was supposed to keep watch so that plague could not sneak across the bar. But was it not foolish to believe he could accomplish that just by himself, and with the help of one station engineer, one boat captain, and two crew members? Fortunately, by April 15th, Astoria's police chief reported 210 dead rats handed in.[121]

[121] Ibid., April 15, 1900 "About the City."

FIFTY THOUSAND JAPANESE ARE BOUND FOR PACIFIC COAST

Celestials Ready to Become Native Sons.

Small Army of Coolies, Bound for California, Landed on Puget Sound in One Week.

Lured to the Occident by Tales of Gold and Loaned Sufficient Money to Permit Them to Enter the Land of Promise.

Special Dispatch to The Call.

Japanese "Students" on the Nippon Maru.

TACOMA, Wash., April 18.—An officer of the steamship Goodwin, which arrived yesterday from Japan, says that a regular emigration craze has taken hold of Japan with respect to the shipment of thousands of young Japanese to the United States. He says eight steamers now due are bringing [illegible] more Japanese to be landed at Seattle and Tacoma within the next week, making [illegible] landed on Puget Sound within a week. His story of the emigration movement in Japan is as follows:

Several score emigration agents are at work among the farming classes in the interior of Japan. They hold out inducements for young men between 19 and 25 to come to America, producing letters from Japanese now in America telling of their prosperity, together with photographs of American scenes. Soon a regular fever to emigrate to the Pacific Coast takes hold of the younger generation. Fathers are then approached and induced to pay or raise $40 to ship their sons across the Pacific. About half of this amount goes to pay transportation and other expenses, the balance of $20 being apparently given to each immigrant to show when he passes inspection on arrival here. The law requires that each immigrant must possess $20.

Landing Money Returned.

As fast as the Japanese have passed inspection when landed at Tacoma they march uptown in military formation. At one of the houses where they are quartered it is said that the $20 shown to the immigration inspectors is returned to an agent and eventually sent back to the emigration company in Japan. Emigration agents in Japan lead Japanese youths to believe that they will get easy positions [illegible] in this country. After landing they find usually that railroad work is ahead of them, but they nevertheless receive the $1 [illegible] a day which they expected as starters. An examination of the several hundred Japanese brought by the Goodwin shows that practically all are under 25 years of age. They are thin but strong enough for heavy work, their weight ranging from 115 to 125 [illegible] main channel of immigration to Puget Sound and California.

Hundreds About Due.

Large shipments of Japanese have arrived on Puget Sound this week per Rio Jun Maru, Milos and the Goodwin. About [illegible] more are coming on the Braemar, due before Saturday. There is reason to believe that emigration agents make at least 50 per cent profit out of the $60 paid them by each immigrant. As near as can be learned the steamship companies receive $15 to $16 per head, making handsome returns for the steamship companies, since the cost of feeding Japanese in parties of a thousand or more does not exceed $1.50 to $2 each. It is noticeable that the Japanese are all dressed alike and most of them carry hand satchels which are also exactly alike. This leads to the conclusion that they are outfitted in Tokio, Yokohama and Kobe by firms which furnish their supplies in wholesale quantities. Allowing $16 for steamship fare and $12 for an outfit, the emigration agent still has $32 left for his own services. A steamship officer who has made public this mode of procedure will not permit the use of his name for obvious reasons. He says that so fully impressed are many farmers with the opportunity to make fortunes afforded their sons in this country that they do not hesitate to mortgage their small plots of ground to raise the necessary $60.

It is noticeable that many Japanese land in Victoria, thence coming across by Sound steamer. This permits Japanese who have landed here to wire or mail their $20 each back to Victoria for the use of other Japanese in passing the immigrant inspector.

VICTORIA, B. C., April 18.—Another thousand Japanese are at the wharf here waiting until the authorities shall allow the steamer Milos, a filthy German tramp, on which they came, to enter. The crowd brought to the Milos brings the total number of arrivals here from Japan since January 1 to 6025. Over 3000 more are on the way to this port, 900 on the steamer Braemar, due here on Monday; 1000 on [illegible] party working down slowly. The railways, too, are employing a great many [illegible] have been crowded. From these two points they slowly work down, most of [illegible] upon to pay 25 cents per day for food. And to the coolie this side of the ocean [illegible] across the border as best they can. They are, too, promised good food on steamers, but on the Milos they were almost starved. The cooks prepared the eternal rice, sometimes with a few small fishes thrown in, and heaped it, boiling in big caldrons on either side of the deck. The closely packed immigrants would fight for positions near the caldrons, and when able grab a handful of rice and would munch it from their fists as they sat about the decks. The Milos is held here not only because of the fact that her captain has no clearance, but also as she has insufficient boats. There are only four for a thousand passengers. The steamer is in a most filthy state, the scuppers being piled up with evil smelling refuse.

Her officers report seeing a dismasted wreck about a thousand miles from Flattery. They passed within nine miles of it.

Group of Chinese on Forward Deck of the Nippon Maru.

NEW SCHEME WORKED BY ARIZONA CHINAMEN

Special Dispatch to The Call.

PHOENIX, Ariz., April 18.—The United States District Attorney of Arizona today received instructions from the Attorney General at Washington to cause the arrest of a Chinaman named Lan Wing Quong, who is now living at Tucson. The case of this Chinaman is one of sensational interest. He came over from China to San Francisco about March 1, where, it is said, he attempted to land. Failing in this he was taken in hand by agents, who had been employed by his father, a wealthy Chinese merchant in Tucson, and given over to the Southern Pacific road, which placed him in bond for Mexico. The father was notified of this action and when the Southern Pacific train reached Tucson with the Chinaman a writ of habeas corpus, which had been issued by Judge George R. Davis of the District bench, was served on the Southern Pacific agent and the Chinaman was delivered to the officers. The hearing on the writ resulted in the discharge of the [illegible] unintentionally fallen into a conspiracy to get this Chinaman into the country and the scheme is regarded as a new and clever dodge of the Chinese exclusion law. This opinion was confirmed to-day by instructions received from the Attorney General. United States Commissioner Culver was at once notified to issue a warrant for the arrest of the Chinaman, but he refused, claiming that Judge Davis had passed on the matter and he did not feel justified in reopening the case.

Assistant United States District Attorney Bennett left to-night for Tucson and the case of Lan Wing Quong will be taken up according to the instructions of the Attorney General.

EXAMINING ASIATICS ON THE NIPPON MARU

Friends Are Kept Away From Them and as Yet None Have Been Landed.

The Chinese and Japanese coolies on the Nippon Maru had a quiet time of it yesterday. After the hurry and rush of going into quarantine at Angel Island, the trip across the bay on the steamer Caroline and the scramble to get aboard the Nippon Maru every one of the Asiatics was ready for a rest.

Yesterday nearly all of them were rehearsing the lesson they have to tell the Commissioner. On the dock were a number of the pigtailed fraternity from Chinatown, who whenever they got a chance shouted to one or another of the passengers, who would answer and then quickly disappear. A number of Japanese attempted to get aboard the steamer on the pretext that they had relatives among the crew, but the customs officers were obdurate and they had to remain ashore.

The work of examining the Japanese began yesterday before the Immigration Commissioner. The statements of quite a number of men were taken, but so far none of them have been landed. The taking of testimony in the case of the Chinese will begin to-day, and after The Call's expose it is safe to say that the evidence will be conclusive before a coolie, be he merchant or native son, can land.

In the pier over the entrance to the Mail dock there is another bunch of Chi-

Dr. Hastings probably slept poorly in April because events and news continued to be contradictable. On April 7th, the cleaning of San Francisco was concluded. Observers held their breath, wondering if it would be effective. On April 16th, Osaka, Japan, reported new cases. From there, it might advance to Hawaii and on to the U.S. West Coast again. It was quickly proven that cleaning up San Francisco without instituting public health measures was not going to eliminate plague from the city. On April 24th, a new case was announced. From Hawaii came the opposite message. On April 26th, government officials announced that the plague seemed to have vanished in Hawaii. From now on U.S. authorities should issue clean bills of health to ships wanting to leave port.[122] Dr. Hastings thought that such a return to normalcy came way too fast. The issuance of a clean bill of health seemed premature. First, he wanted a city to show thirty days without incident.[123] Surgeon General Wyman, too, was leaning his way but did not say so in public. He decided to travel to Honolulu to see for himself whether the disease was present or not.

Astoria's business community pushed such news aside and focused on the opening of salmon season on April 15th at noon. Most Finish sailors arrived by the end of the second week of April. During the next two weeks, they pulled their vessels out of storage and outfitted them.[124] Three thousand fishermen climbed into 1,500 boats, ready to become the butterfly fleet once again.[125] It was the penultimate year when they caught fish while sailing. In two years, outboard engines would rip open the inspiring mood of the bay with unprecedented gasoline noise. Chinese exclusion laws made the recruitment of cheap Chinese laborers noticeably difficult. This year a thirty percent decline in Chinese laborers in the fish industry was reported.[126] On April 10th, the OR&N's *B.S.*

122 Ibid., April 26, 1900 "About the City."

123 Ibid., April 27,1900, "About the City."

124 LOC, Chronicling America, *The Morning Astorian*, April 11, 1900.

125 Ibid., April 28, 1900.

126 *ADB*, May 1, 1901 "About the City."; and *ADB* March 14, 1900. The pay is $1.25 a day, or $175 to $200 a season. The hours they need to work a day is 11 hours.

ANTI-CHINESE AND ANTI-JAPANESE ARTICLE ABOUT LACK OF WORKERS AND NEW ARRIVALS IN SEATTLE, ASTORIA AND SAN FRANCISCO.

Braemar brought from Yokohama 940 Japanese but only ninety Chinese workers.[127] In Victoria, they were quarantined, but not in Astoria.[128]

Since in Astoria everything was "still fine in port," Astoria's boosters kept boosting. "Wheat, wheat, wheat!" continued to be the loudest wish, expressing a yearning for irrational riches. In Frankfurt, Washington, two bays east of the still mothballed quarantine station in March 1900, a survey was supposed to begin on behalf of the Columbia River Valley Railroad. Only a fifteen-mile gap remained to be closed between Frankfort (a town that has disappeared today) and Cathlamet. Once closed, the mouth of the Columbia would be connected by a straight rail line from Wallula, Washington, to Frankfort, Washington.[129] City boosters predicted the arrival of graders who would cut down the forest and then build a bed for the rail line to Frankfort.[130] Then, in theory, Frankfort could become a major grain exporting location. Not surprisingly, nobody asked if it made sense to operate a large port for exporting grain only 500 yards from a quarantine station where seriously ill people might be waiting to heal.

The commercial fever increased further in temperature when A. M. Hammond interjected himself into dreams of wheat export. He asked to focus on Astoria, Oregon but not Frankfort, Washington. He opined that if warehouses were constructed in Astoria, grain freighters could save a 200-mile trip to Portland and load wheat in Astoria as cheaply as in Portland.

127 Ibid., *ADB*, April 10, 1901. "About the City."

128 Ibid., April 25, 1900,"About the City." LOC, Chronicling America, *The Morning Astorian*, "About the City."

129 A newspaper article mentioned possibility number two: building a bridge across the Columbia to bring wheat to Frankfort.

130 LOC, Chronicling America, *The Morning Astorian*, March 18, 1900, "About the City." But until summer nothing happened. Harriman simply continued the price war on the Oregon side not willing to have his territory being invaded by Hammond's friends. The particular nastiness of his strategy consisted of hoping to bankrupt Hammond and his associated financial backers. Another dream of exporting wheat was tied to the Central Navigation Company that was continuing to build a portage road near the Dalles again offering a boat line from inland wheat fields to the coast.

THE STEEL BARQUE *VINCENNES*. AT DOCK ON THE COLUMBIA RIVER, PORTLAND, OREGON.

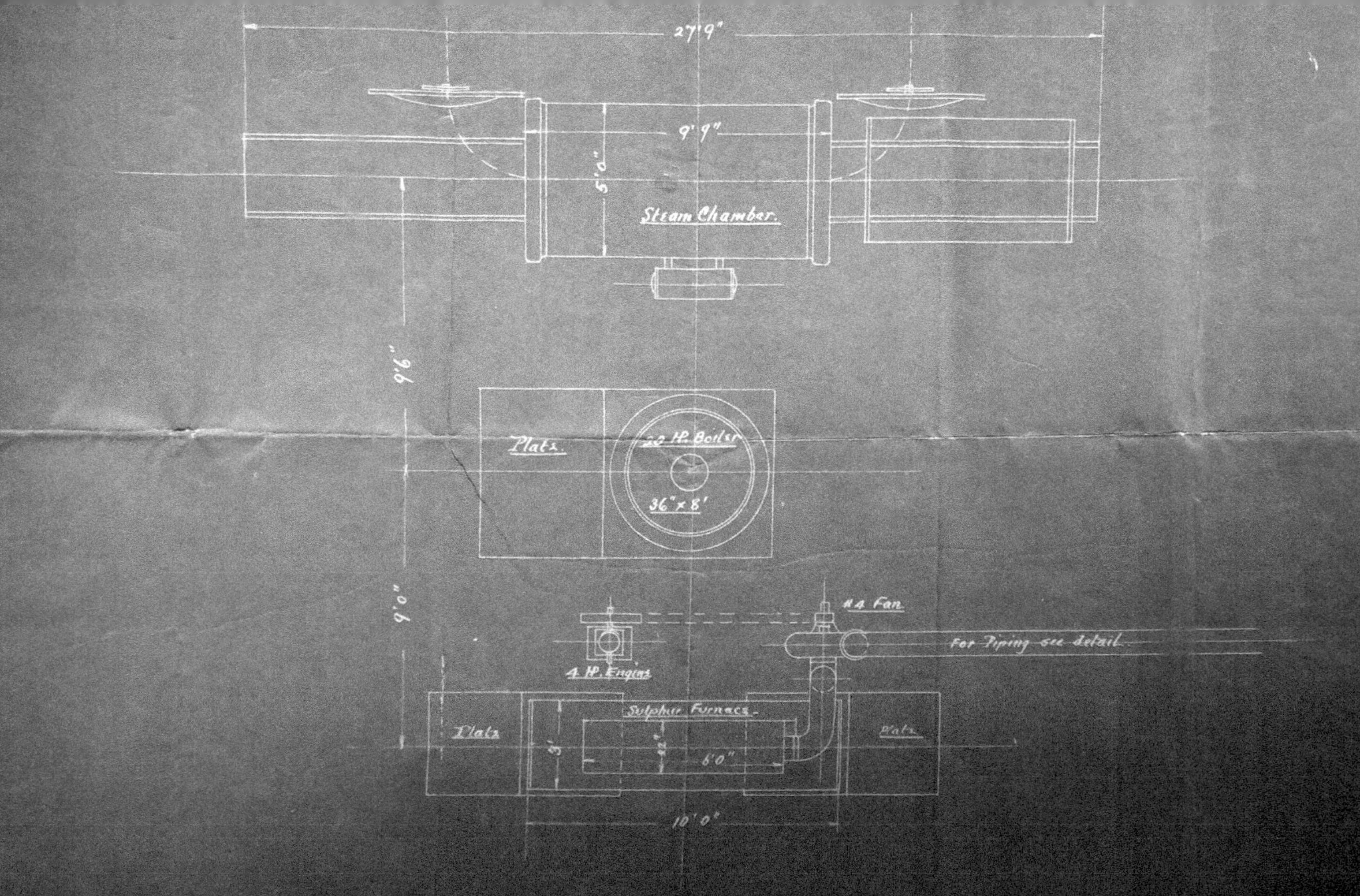

SKETCH OF DISINFECTING MACHINERY.

But first, Hammond wanted to favor lumber over wheat. That meant building a lumber mill to make wood products for export. He was hoping to open a mill creating 200,000 board feet a day. Then he fantasized about using the lumber to increase shipbuilding in Astoria. By March, Hammond bought 400 feet of land from F. H. Smith and Alfred Kinney for $6,500.[131] In the same month, he even visited Astoria. In town, he reassured everybody that Astoria would develop normally. However, he said there was no need to create a rush that did not help.[132] The date for signing would be January 1st, 1901.[133] Not surprisingly Dr. Fulton's brother G. C. Fulton performed part of the legal work.

Independent European shipping companies also knew about opportunities along the river. They sailed to Astoria and Portland, hoping to catch a load. For example, the German Rickmers fleet sent ships. Usually, they traveled from Hamburg to Asia to carry rice to Europe. But in 1900, the Dutch–British war in Southern Africa increased freight rates by two shillings, enough to make a profit if Rickmer's ships returned to Hamburg by crossing the Pacific, stopping in Astoria to load wheat in Portland, and heading home around South America.[134]

In the midst of this, it was confirmed that, on May 5th, the newly built Kensington fumigation chambers left Philadelphia by train. They were expected to arrive in Astoria around May 15th. Then they would be stored on the city's wharf until the cannery remodeling was completed.[135] Dr. Hastings was even comfortable suggesting mid–July 1900 as a potential opening time. Even better,

131 Astoria, Astoria Public Library, *ADB* March 10, 1901, "About the City.".
132 Ibid., , March 12, 1901, "About the City."
133 Ibid., January 16, 1901, "About the City."
134 Rick Rickmer's book. *ADB*, May 1, 1900. Astoria's politicians focused on their sour relationship with Portland's business community. In April 1900 a special committee met trying to find a way to challenge Union Pacific Railroad because it had expanded into Seattle and San Francisco but not into Astoria. *ADB*, December 6, "About the City." Portland's business looked forward to increasing profit using the Oregon Oriental steamship company and *ADB* , Jan 15, 1900, "About the City." The Portland Asiatic Steamship Company, promising increased direct traffic from Asia to the Columbia River, *ADB* Jan 3rd, "About the City."
135 *ADB*, May 9, 1901, "About the City."

SKETCH OF DISINFECTING MACHINERY.

YOW YUEN

finally, the Department of Treasury allowed Hastings to ask for bids from May 28th.[136] Until the cannery's construction, only the most urgent cases would be anchored at the old existing wharf.[137]

In contrast, Dr. Fulton's ability to act independently from Dr. Hastings shrunk. The skipper he sometimes used died. Suddenly, as he became more standoffish to Hastings, he was without transportation.[138] Hastings still had the *Electric* to reach incoming ships.

January to April taught Hastings how little nature's cycles were impressed by the good intentions of doctors eager to heal. Nature was impossible to corral into the longing of humans to create a predictable daily life. But nature was not mean. Humans, in contrast, could be mean. Events during four weeks of May, 1900 became a lesson for Dr. Hastings. He learned how local businesses and politicians could turn against the doctor of a USPHS station and drive him out of town for no other reason than profit. A local community and its commercial priorities could be like a tiger whose unique energies the national public health officer could not tame, even with science on his side. Hastings learned how in San Francisco station leader Dr. Kinyoun was publicly vilified and dangled in political winds at great personal cost.

After weeks without new cases, San Francisco again admitted new plague cases by mid-May. Nine new deaths were counted. Even worse, one person seemed to have carried plague from Sacramento to San Francisco, suggesting that the disease had continued its march from San Francisco into the rest of California. The city's commercial interests, the board of trade, and the shipper's association feared that any day national health experts would impose a quarantine this time over all of San Francisco. One potential way out seemed to be to convince the public through insistent

136 *ADB*, May 1, 1901 "About the City." They should measure 100 x 30 and 250 x 60. One side was to house the disinfection plant, the other bath rooms and laundry.

137 *ADB*, May 1, 1901, "About the City."

138 *ADB*, May 24, 1900, "About the City." Besserich was an immigrant from Austria and had lived in Astoria at least since 1880. *ADB*, June 13, 1900, "About the City." On June 13, Cosmo Franciscovich was appointed by Governor Greer to follow him. He would be paid $500 a year.

propaganda that, after all, no plague was present. Business leaders reached out to California Governor Gage, asking him to create a misleading news cycle. The governor, in turn, hired an incompetent friend, Dr. Winston Anderson, to conduct an investigation to produce the desired lie.

In Washington, D.C., Surgeon General Wyman feared the worst. On May 15th, he predicted that the local presence of plague would grow into a regional epidemic. Right away, he counseled vaccination and shipped 22,000 doses of serum to San Francisco. He asked city leaders to enact some kind of vaccination plan, and, on May 19th, he offered free inoculations. However, instead of launching an all-encompassing public health campaign, Californians only rented an island where future diseased people could be quarantined and, more than likely, die.

President McKinley still backed his surgeon general. Both men asked Dr. Kinyoun to execute the government's orders. Dr. Kinyoun was not happy with what he was asked to do. He interpreted the orders as "drastic in their character, in many ways impractical regulations that could be enforced only with hardship." And yet, a quarantine was imposed over San Francisco. The doctor of the USPHS did what his oath of office asked him to do.

None of this mattered to San Francisco activists battling for principled respect for Chinese Americans. Surprisingly, the railroad companies found themselves on their side as they challenged the surgeon general's orders as racist and unconstitutional in court Together they enlisted courts to rescind the blanket quarantine order so that no single act should be undertaken that targeted only individuals of Chinese background. A short while thereafter, a judge agreed that Washington's orders were based on "race" alone. Surgeon General Wyman was ordered to end all and any violation of the constitution in San Francisco. The law trumped quarantine measures even during a plague epidemic.

Dr. Kinyoun's stress level increased further because 1900 was a presidential election year. Politics being politics, now U.S.

WALTER WYMAN, 3RD SURGEON GENERAL OF THE UNITED STATES (1891-1911).

President McKinley seemed to step back a bit from his passionate and accomplished Surgeon General Wyman and his station head Dr. Kinyoun in San Francisco. From afar, President McKinley's political rivals, the Republican Party, used the serious emergency in California to score political points in preparation for the upcoming November election day.

Dr. Wyman reacted by throwing against manipulations a counter-publicity campaign. From N. Y., he dispatched Dr. Geo Shrady, a journalist, to San Francisco. He was to look at all available evidence and report if facts showed that plague existed in San Francisco. On May 22nd, Dr. Shrady confirmed in a newspaper article the presence of plague. Furthermore he agreed that it was spreading. He was unskilled in messaging politically complicated issues to a by now panicked public. He poured gasoline onto racist fires when he proclaimed that only the destruction of Chinatown might eliminate the danger.[139] It seemed as if the events of Honolulu might repeat in California.

Even though the court ended broad quarantine, political vitriol in California continued. Now a scapegoat had to be found, and California politicians zeroed in on Dr. Kinyoun, the person who enacted the rescinded measure. A political vendetta campaign aimed to have him fired. From afar, Dr. Hastings observed how, under the right circumstances, politicians could fire a much-accomplished national health leader who had just recently founded the precursor of the U. S. National Institute of Health. So far, in Astoria, the local and regional political establishment had not turned against the head of the Columbia River Quarantine station. Dr. Hastings was still respected by the local medical community. Oregon was not California, not yet.

Hastings was pulled into events in California in more than one way. Surgeon General Wyman asked Dr. Kinyoun to take over the leadership of anti-plague measures along the entire U. S. west coast. Suddenly, Dr. Kinyoun was Dr. Hastings's superior. Almost

[139] NLM, Joseph Kinyoun papers, "to my dear Aunt and Uncle, Detroit, June 29th 1901." Accessed January 2nd, 2022.

the station in Astoria was a branch of San Francisco's network as far as a plague campaign was concerned. In order to help with the increased workload, Washington, D.C. gave Dr. Kinyoun ten new assistants.[140] Strangely, none of them were dispatched to Dr. Hastings in Astoria.

That week, the year's first strawberries were offered at Foard and Stoke's. Nevertheless, this was no time for a fragrant culinary delight for Hastings. To the contrary, a test of political power between Oregon and the national representatives was looming.

First, as far as plague in Hawaii was concerned, Washington, D.C. ordered him on May 18th to end stopping the principled fumigation of ships coming from Hawaii. From then on, fumigation was declared necessary only when a sick person was found on board.[141] However, as far as the plague in San Francisco was concerned, Oregon's Dr. Fulton instituted rules that Washington, D.C. had not issued. On May 18th, he decreed that all ships arriving from San Francisco would have to quarantine at the lower part of the bay. Also, all trains coming from San Francisco were to be quarantined.[142]

Since Hastings tried to play matters by the book, he refused to follow Fulton's order arguing that he had not received an official notification from Washington, D.C.[143] Fulton wired to Washington, D.C. for direction, asking Wyman if in San Francisco an official plague emergency was existing.[144] It was frustrating that Wyman did not telegraph a response. Until May 20th, the official position remained that there was no plague in California.[145]

Dr. Hastings attempted not to be in open and direct opposition to Fulton and at least to offer a gesture of tolerance. An open break was prevented as Fulton and Hastings agreed to declare the lower end of the river a zone of quarantine and to keep vessels there.[146]

140 NLM, Kinyoun Papers, "Letter to Uncle and Aunt 1901."
141 *ADB*, May 18, 1900, "About the City."
142 LOC, *The Morning Astorian*, May 20, 1900 image 3.
143 *ADB*, April 20, "About the City."
144 *ADB* May 18, 1900, "About the City."
145 *ADB* May 21, 1900, "About the City."
146 *ADB*, May 20, 1901. "About the City."

FOARD & STOKES CO.

DEALERS IN

Naval Supplies

Ship Chandlery

FISHBOAT AND YACHT SUPPLIES

FRESH VEGETABLES AND FISH.

❧

Anything from a Needle to an Anchor.

ASTORIA, OREGON.

[12]
False Alarm: the First Two "Cases" at the Station

SUDDENLY THE NEXT DAY, May 21st, the official line from San Francisco changed, and Hastings and Fulton were notified that plague was present in San Francisco.[147]

On that same day, Hastings and Fulton were forced to face what they had feared for a long time. From San Francisco, the *SS Columbia* arrived, bringing along two individuals suspected of carrying plague. [148] Even though the construction and transformation of the station were not finished, Dr. Hastings decided to place two individuals into the mothballed cannery across the bay. Suddenly "quarantine procedure" was no longer a quick forty-eight-hour process of hooking up pipes and running steam through them. Now it was dealing with people potentially carrying a real, most dangerous pathogen inside the bay. [149]

In Astoria, Dr. Kinney's voice again pointed to this debate's truth. He insisted that the disease would be brought to Astoria by rats, not Chinese people.[150] Second, Dr. Kinney suggested increasing the bounty for a rat turned in. The funds to accomplish this increase had to be found outside the city budget. Kinney raised the funds, and the city was able to double the reward from five to ten cents per rat.[151]

---

147 *ADB*, May 21, 1901. "About the City."
148 *ADB*, May 21, 1901. "About the City."
149 *ADB*, May 21, 1900. "About the City." The records list them based on Chinese ethnicity, not based on being human with names.
150 *ADB*, May 5, 1900, "About the City."
151 *ADB*, May 22, 1900, "About the City."

FOARD AND STOKES CO. NAVAL SUPPLIES.

Public health rules in town also improved. More sophisticated guidelines detailed better ways to drop off a rat. It sunk in that touching a dead rat infected with fleas was not only a really bad idea but, potentially, a ticket to death. Updated rules advised finders not to use a hand but a stick to touch the rat. Furthermore, finders should bring dead rats to the police station in a paper bag.[152] This was appropriate advice because rats kept coming. By May 29th, the number of rats dropped off reached 300.[153] Kinney added the order to burn rats found on ships. They must never be allowed to leave the vessel.[154]

The sources do not tell us if and how Hastings communicated to the community the presence of two people potentially ill with plague. Could this have remained a secret in such a small, close-knit community?

They were expected to be released on June 1st. Suddenly their presence became an immigration question. Hastings agreed with immigration inspector McLean that the papers of the two men might not be in regular order. McLean and Hastings investigated their papers to decide whether Fox needed to be informed. When their papers proved fine, the men were released and allowed to proceed to Portland.[155]

---

[152] *ADB*, May 22, 1900, "About the City."

[153] *ADB*, May 29, 1900, "About the City."

[154] *ADB*, June 23, 1900, "About the City." *ADB*, June 1, 1900, "About the City." Weather was excellent that day and one could see the station across the bay. There the two passengers from the SS Columbia were still in quarantine. *ADB* June 14, 1900. "About the City.

[155] *ADB*, June 14, 1900, "About the City."

SS Columbia under full sail.

[13]

Hill Hastings is Pulled Into the Orbit of San Francisco's Plague Crisis

CALIFORNIA EVENTS IMPACTED OREGON a second time. In order to keep plague bottled up, Dr. Kinyoun used the public declaration of plague to attempt to bottle it up inside the city and the state by creating new tools. This time, he invented the use of a domestic health certificate for ships departing from San Francisco to other U.S. ports. All ships now had to show such a health certificate, which usually only ships from abroad had to do. Within ten days U.S. health officers inspected all passengers boarding a vessel. And again, a "racial" lens was applied. Any boat carrying Japanese or Chinese passengers was prohibited from leaving.[156] Second, Washington, D.C. imposed strict rules along the California and Oregon border. Acting Assistant Surgeon General McGreer ordered inspections of all passengers that arrived from California.[157]

To say it differently, one month after the kickoff of Astoria's fishing season, ethnically Japanese and Chinese individuals could no longer reach Astoria by boat. Perhaps Kinyoun's action kept Hastings and Fulton from clashing openly about how to treat incoming ships from San Francisco. For the time being, Kinyoun's order made the essence of the conflict between Dr. Fulton and Dr.

156 *ADB*, June 5, 1900, "About the City."
157 *ADB*, May 22, 1900, "About the City."

RAT'S NEST IN A SHOE, HANDED IN IN SAN FRANCISCO.

Hastings mute. Also, the two quarantined men sitting inside the cannery proved not to have plague and could be released.

Elsewhere along the west coast, the culture wars over plague refused to disappear. On June 18th, the quarantine over San Francisco's Chinatown was lifted by court decree. In Seattle, two men arriving from San Francisco were arrested. In Astoria, Dr. Henderson embarked on yet another cleaning campaign. It covered all of the city superficially, but when he came to Chinatown, he examined every house in detail. What he found to his dislike, he ordered to be cleaned.[158]

In Salem, observers realized that Oregon Governor Greer lacked the legal tools to decree the quarantine of individuals for the entire state. Only in Yaquina and Astoria did the presence of an Oregon health officer offer the possibility to shut down a town. Therefore, Dr. Fulton used a presentation at a medical convention to advocate the creation of an Oregon Board of Health that should gain the power to impose a quarantine on all of Oregon.[159] Others strongly endorsed his suggestion, and a legislative committee was tasked to create a bill that would give the governor this right if necessary. [160] Similar suggestions were debated in the state of Washington, where the governor wanted to impose quarantine over the entire state as well.

In San Francisco, Dr. Kinyoun was now a personal target, very much like Dr. Fauci became a target of anti-vaxxers in 2021. On June 16th, one publication published images of the board of health and Dr. Kinyoun stating, "these men are marked." [161] Somehow Dr. Kinyoun was supposed to be driven out of town and his job. In Astoria, the truce between Fulton and Hastings held. A direct open, ongoing battle between the USPHS and Oregon state representatives continued to be avoided.

[158] *ADB*, May 22, 1900 "About the City."
[159] *ADB*, June 27, 1900, "About the City."
[160] *ADB*, June 27, 1900, "About the City."
[161] NLM, Joseph Kinyoun papers, "to my dear Aunt and Uncle, Detroit, June 29th 1901." Accessed January 2nd, 2022.

[14] Getting Physical: Sawing and Hammering at the Cannery

DURING THIS TENSE ENVIRONMENT, the Kensington fumigation machinery arrived from Philadelphia on May 22nd. It was parked on the OR&N dock. The Department of Treasury approved hiring a supervising architect on May 28th. The company that received the winning bid belonged to Astoria's mayor Suprenant.[162] But right away, he subcontracted the work to Leander Lebeck, who coincidentally lived on the OR&N dock close to where the fumigation machine was waiting.[163] Hill Hastings was thrilled that he could finally act. He ordered newly lumbered boards, fresh paint, and nails to be put on a boat and shipped across the bay to the cannery. Finally, Hume's cannery was becoming the USPHS quarantine station.[164]

Lebeck's first planned construction was a new wharf. It would measure 250 feet in length and sixty feet in width. Located 650 feet out from shore, it offered a constant depth of twenty-three feet, sufficient to keep an ocean-going vessel afloat, even at low tide. This new wharf would stand in the river within sixty days.[165]

162 NARA, RG 90, Treasury Department, Supervising Architect, June 14, 1900.
163 *ADB*, June 7, 1900, " About the City."
164 *ADB*. A second source dated the arrival of the fumigation equipment to May 28.
165 LOC, Morning Astorian, My 2nd, 1900.

Residence Phone Black 2193

LEANDER LEBECK

House Moving,
Bridge Building,
Pile Driving, Wharf Work
And General Contracting.

OFFICE:	RESIDENCE:
522 BOND STREET	323 COLUMBIA AV.

ASTORIA, OREGON.

Before construction could begin, Dr. Hastings requested money to produce a chart and plan of the station's property.

> *...it is desirable that is being created an accurate knowledge of the property, both of the shore and water to the channel, to know as surveyed the proper location of the new structures.*[166]

Such a survey would pinpoint how to install the new wharf at a proper angle and in the middle of the property. R. C. Astburg, Leander Lebeck's foreman, offered to perform the survey for $28. Once again, written approval from the Office of the Superintendent of Construction in D. C. was the first step.[167]

In the meantime, Dr. Hastings started a third round of hiring. This time he assembled a construction crew. By May 21st, an unspecified position had been filled by W. F. Binder. Then, Hastings hired Mr. Ball as the foreman of construction. Ole Estoos filled a carpenter position.

On June 7th, from Washington, D. C., Acting Secretary of the Treasury Spelding approved the $9,800 bid for the new wharf.[168] Right away, Lebeck moved the pile driver across the bay. On June 27th, Astburg surveyed the property and established the true northern and southern boundaries and their relationship to the North Pacific Improvement Company.[169] Then the first pilings went into the mud barely a hundred yards away from the Washington shore.[170] Later, Leander Lebeck would subcontract braces on the new wharf and the construction of a roadway to the station.[171]

---

166 NARA, Hill Hastings to SSG Wash D. C. May 21, 1900.

167 NARA, Hill Hastings to Surgeon General, July 5, 1900.

168 *ADB*, June 13, 1900, "About the City."

169 NARA, RG 90, letter, Foreman Ball to Dr. Hill Hastings, July 5, 1900. Hastings also wanted to recover repair costs of $170.31. Talks continued going back and forth about who should bear all expense rising from necessary repairs to keep the boat in good condition.

170 *ADB* June 28, 1900, "About the City."

171 His real name was Leander Lebeck born September 4, 1863. His wife was Milka Johanna Vilhelmsdr. In town she called herself Millie Wilson. His party affiliation was Democrat. His political work brought him close to Alfred Kinney. In 1901 he had also bet on work for 31st Street.

ADVERTISEMENT. LEANDER LEBECK WAS THE LEADING CONTRACTOR DOING WHARF AND BUILDING WORK.

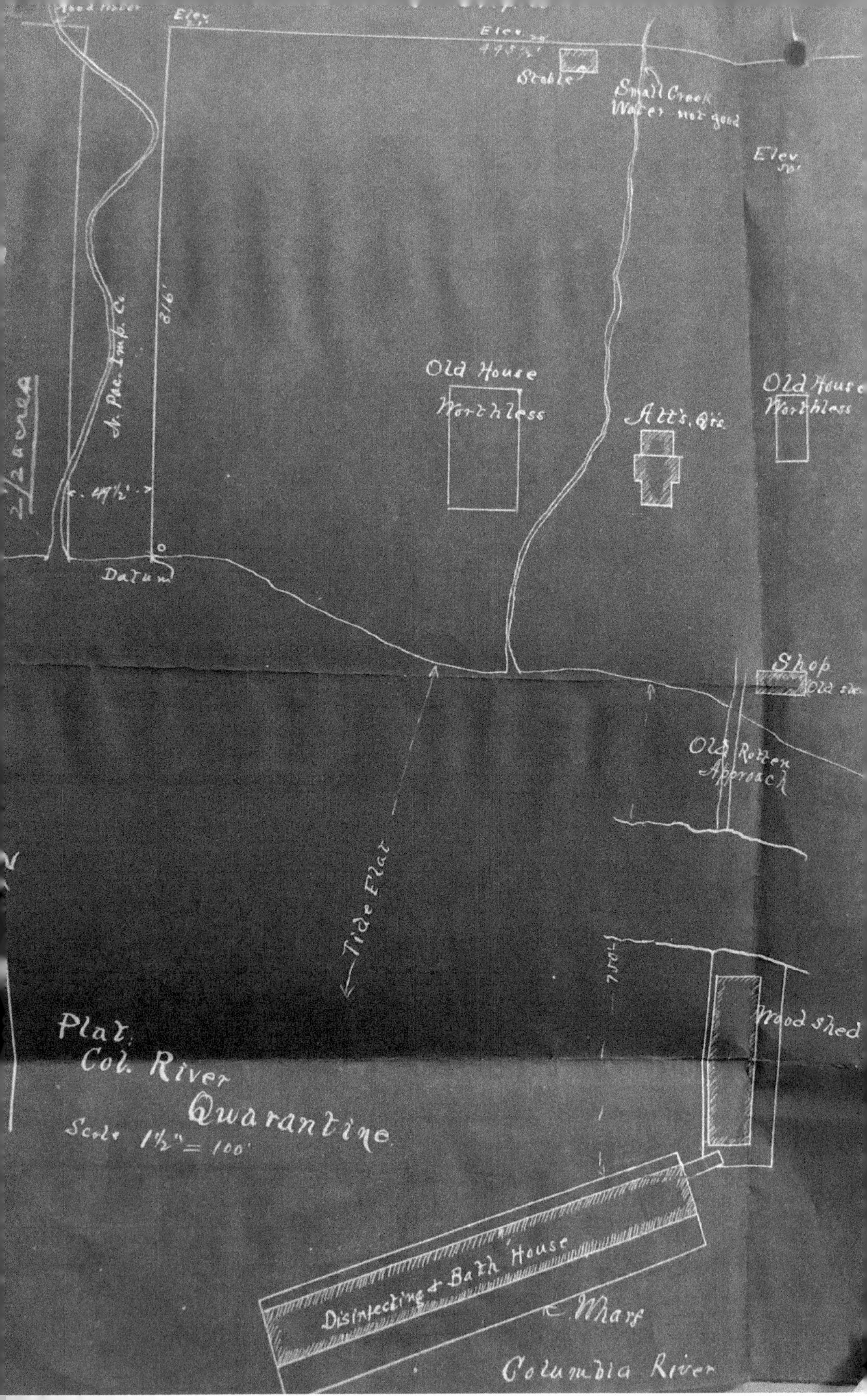

Plat
Col. River
Quarantine
Scale 1½" = 100'

Elev.
Elev.
Elev. 50'
Stable
Small Creek
Water not good
N. Pac. Imp. Co.
816'
44½'
2½ acres
Datum
Old House
Worthless
Att's. Qrs.
Old House
Worthless
Shop
Old shed
Old Rotten
Approach
Tide Flat
750'
Wood shed
Disinfecting & Bath House
Wharf
Columbia River

Finally, Dr. Hastings was able to order supplies from Astoria's Fisher Brothers. Delivery was scheduled to take place during the first week of July.[172] Now Hastings mentioned a more specific opening date: someday in mid-August.

The work specified needed to be done not only on the buildings but also on Hastings's means of transportation. Hastings's contract with Babbidge to use the *Electric* was to expire on August 10th. When negotiations began, Babbidge proposed to increase the monthly rent for the *Electric* to $200. [173] In addition, he wanted thirty dollars per month to cover the cost of keeping the boat in good condition aside from the cost of repairs to machinery. This included beaching the vessel twice a year to clean the hull and caulking it once a year. Then he made an ominous announcement. Babbidge wanted the new contract to include a paragraph that gave him the right to sell the *Electric,* provided he could furnish an acceptable replacement vessel. What else could Dr. Hastings do besides agree to Babbidge's proposal of a four-month project extension?[174] He had not even begun negotiating a boat construction on an Astorian boatyard.

And so, work began. The survey showed obvious repairs. The dock needed to be installed at the proper angle and in the middle of the property. After that, mooring dolphins should be placed on government property. These priorities addressed key issues only outside the buildings. Quickly, attention turned to existing and future buildings. $3,450 was to be spent to repair existing buildings in August. The old dock was to be stabilized and a safe approach from the wharf to shore was to be built. Old buildings had to be made weather tight, so they could be used at least as temporary barracks for disinfection until a new one had been built.[175]

The USPHS wondered what to do with the larger house that stood on the land. Originally, it was designated to house attendants.

172 *ADB*, July 7, 1900, "About the City."
173 Contract talks began June 9.
174 LOC, Morning Astorian, October 7, 1900.
175 NARA, RG 90, Hastings to SSG, December 4, 1900.

THE ORIGINAL PLAT MAP OF THE TERRITORY OF THE STATION.

HARDWARE

However, an examination discovered that it was in such a poor state that it was razed.

Then, a new, very substantial six-room house was constructed to house future attendants. It would have three rooms on the second floor, a ground-floor living room, facilities, and a sitting room. Also, it would offer a kitchen that could be used.

After dealing with the wharf and transportation, Dr. Hastings turned to making the station and future building operable and livable. That meant securing access to a reliable water source. For that purpose, a 3,000-gallon water tank was to be built, where fresh water could be piped to the new wharf and the yet-to-be-built houses on the land. Piping had to be laid to connect the tank and wharf. A second set of pipes was to carry sewage away from the property.[176]

Finally, the new station needed to be marked better. Currently, three spare buoys marked the channel opposite the station. One was 1,000 feet opposite the disinfecting wharf, a second was 1.8 miles below, and a third was 1.6 miles above the wharf. The buoys marked a channel 1,000 to 1,500 feet wide and twenty-five to thirty-five feet deep.

As important as hiring an engineer was, hiring a person who would attend to the needs of future arriving female passengers. Annie Abraham would become that person in 1901. She was born Annie Gaberg in Norway in 1865.[177] Emigration records in Trondheim tell us that she left Norway and arrived in the U.S. at the latest in 1882. Like thousands of other women, she made her way to the Northwest via Michigan and Wisconsin. On the way, her daughter Ovidia was born, and she married her first husband, Mr. Wiggin. By 1886 she had arrived opposite the station in Clatsop County. For unknown reasons, she married a second time in November 1886. Two years later, she and her new husband,

[176] NARA, RG 90, Hastings. A report informed Washington that these repairs would be enough to provide the station with the necessary improvements for the operation of the station winter 1900-1901.

[177] The following story based on her personal data is excerpted from a posted chat on forum.arkivverket.no.accessed October 23, 2021.

Samual Abraham,[178] became parents to their son, Frank Albert. Then, in 1900, Samuel Abraham suddenly died. Dr. Hastings might have heard of her then as a sudden widow living close to the station and caring for two children alone.[179]

Finally, Hastings received a letter to examine and certify Thaddeus Trullinger as the station's engineer. On October 26, 1900, he reported that this was accomplished. Trullinger's probationary working period began.

During those weeks, a colleague pointed out to Dr. Hastings that an opening would soon occur in the Los Angeles office. Officially, Hastings shared that he was suffering from neuralgia and rheumatism, and California's warm weather would certainly help with these conditions. Eighteen months after arriving in Oregon, Hill Hastings learned that the USPHS would accept his application for the California position. He would spend Christmas in the warmer southern U. S.

---

178 Marriage Certificate, State of Oregon, County of Clatsop, Astoria, recorded December 4th, 1886. And Affidavit of Marriage License. Ibid.

179 A sincere thank you to Nancy Anderson, Heather Henry, and Penny Kramer of the Pacific County Historical Society for help in finding records.

A WOMAN AND A BOY WALK ALONG THE BOARDWALK CONNECTING KNAPPTON AND THE STATION.

[15]

An Open Station: No Longer a Cannery!

IN THE LAST WEEK of September, Dr. Joseph M. J. Kingmar came from Seattle to Astoria to inspect the new repairs, and probably, to commission the station. On September 27th, he approved the construction and opening of buildings Dr. Hastings had been responsible for.[180] Now, Astoria had a fully functioning separate space where ships could dock, people could be treated, and suitcases fumigated. The time when ships had to stop within yards of Astoria's wharf was coming to an end.

And yet, construction continued. Additional smaller buildings were constructed in the bay. On October 1st, Hastings sent a group of men to the station and construction commenced on October 8th.[181] Also, in mid-October, the channel next to the station was measured again by bar pilots.[182] When even this work was finished, Dr. Hastings cabled to Surgeon General Wyman proudly:

> *I have the honor to report that this station is now equipped and ready for the disinfection of vessels, effects of passengers and crew and provided with ample facilities for bathing all persons aboard ship. The two steam chambers and formalin attachments two boilers bi-chlorid pump sulfur furnace and fan, all are in good and convenient working order. The water supply just completed, is excellent and the hot water heater*

180 Astoria Public Library, Leissenaar Collection, APL 25000, Box 1.
181 LOC, Morning Astorian, October 2nd.
182 LOC, *Morning Astorian*, October 14, 1900.

THE NEW WHARF AND BUILDINGS
LEBECK BUILT.

is sufficient to run the 15 shower sprinklers of the bathhouse. The wharf and buildings are completed in accordance with the contract and are amply large and commodious.[183]

Very rarely, Hastings processed immigrants staying in Astoria. On September 2nd, he processed one person of Chinese ancestry and one of European ancestry. In December 1900, he processed seven individuals.

In contrast to the tohuwabohu unfolding in San Francisco, there hovered a strange pregnant silence over Astoria's Bay. Even though plague could still come from San Francisco and Dr. Fulton remained eager to clamp down on imaginary ill arrivals, he had to admit that all fifty-two ships entering between October 1st and December 31st would be certified in good health.[184]

In the last half of the year, Dr. Hastings supervised installing fumigation technology, constructing a new wharf, and converting existing buildings into buildings for new use. He built two new structures and secured the shipping lanes to the new wharf. What needs to be added to an overview of his tasks is a short exploration of treating the ballast of ships. Not only crews, passengers, suitcases, or cargo but also rocks and mud resting at the bottom of a ship could relocate a virus or a bacterium across the world.

183 NARA, RG 90, Hill Hastings to SSG November 18, 1900.
184 LOC, *The Morning Astorian*, January 5, 1901.

STEAM STERILIZERS IN THE DELOUSING BUILDING. NOTE HOW THE CLOTHING IS HUNG FROM HOOKS AND HANGERS. AT THE LEFT, A REVOLVING DRUM THROUGH WHICH THE CLOTHING IS PASSED INTO THE DRESSING OR UNDRESSING ROOM.

[16]
The Big Deal That Ballast Is

WHO KNEW THAT THERE was so much to ballast? British ships were known to be rather casual when loading weight into a ship's bottom. It was not unheard of that British ballast moved during a ship's journey, decentered the vessel, and made it arrive with a list. The *Falklandback* struggled this way into Astoria.[185] In contrast, contemporaries praised French captains and their ballast work. Different ports packed ballast differently. For example, in Santa Rosalia, Mexico, ballast was dredged out of the harbor bottom and immediately placed in a very wet state into a ship's hull. Not surprisingly, Santa Rosalia mud, too, tended to shift, destabilizing ships trying to cut through waves.

Ballast could even be good. When the *Mahukona* discharged rocks, J. Lindenburger was waiting in Astoria to use it to construct a new private wharf.

The most problematic ballast came from Shanghai. Because cholera raged in this city, mud from Shanghai's port could contain live cholera bacteria. When Shanghai mud arrived in Astoria, Dr. Hastings and his successor had to keep this potentially infected earth away from Astoria's bay front. Curiously nobody minded that it was treated on the Washington side and then dumped into the river.

What that meant was illustrated by the example of the sailing ship *County of Roxborough*. For that story, we must jump ahead one year to October 24th, 1901, when Captain Leslie steered the *County of Roxborough* into port.[186] She had come to load wheat and

185 LOC, *Morning Astorian*, 1901, December 15, 1901. This took place one year later in 1901.

186 LOC, Morning Astorian, October 26, 1902. Two men deserted on November 7. LOC, *The Morning Astorian*, November 13, image 3.

SHOWER AND BATH FACILITY INSIDE THE STATION.

then continue to Europe.

The captain's health report listed one male crew member sick on board with Cholera during the early stage of the trip. But he had died rapidly. Now the bill of health "suggested the possibility that somehow cholera might still be present on board." Right away, the *County of Roxborough* was towed across the river to be put in quarantine along the station's wharf. Washington, D. C. ordered the ballast to be dug out and fumigated. The *Morning Astorian* called this "one of the most unique cases that has ever come up on the coast."[187] Overnight, the head of the quarantine station had to find a way to pump an acidic solution into the 1, 050 feet of mud inside the ship's hull and later discharge it into the bay. Much of it still rests there today in its disinfected state.

Supervising this task was engineer Thaddeus Trullinger. Also, the *County of Roxborough* crew was supposed to stay in quarantine and help. However, four sailors decided to run away. Now treating and excavations took longer. At the very end, it would be November 23rd to have the ballast treated and excavated. The *County of Roxborough* left the USPHS quarantine on November 25th, crossed the river, and anchored below Smith's point.[188] Ballast was a major but overlooked task a station's doctor had to deal with.

Dr. Hastings's term was certainly coming to an end. On November 24th, Dr. Baylis H. Earle, currently serving in Nome, Alaska, as part of Dr. Kinyoun's west coast anti-plague team, was announced as Dr. Hastings's replacement.[189] On December 3rd, records place Dr. Earle in Astoria. Five days later, he reported for work and joined Dr. Hastings. This handover was to conclude on December 12th, the day Hastings was scheduled to leave.[190]

---

[187] LOC, Morning Astorian, October 28, 1901.

[188] Sometimes in ballast cases the pump broke down. Even though it potentially processed cholera infested mud it was carried into Astoria to be repaired with bare hands.

[189] LOC, *Morning Astorian*, December 4, 1900.

[190] LOC, *Morning Astorian*, December 13, 1900.

A TUG PULLS THE *COUNTY OF ROXBOROUGH* IN PREPARATION OF BALLAST EXCAVATION WORK.

[17] Hill Hastings's Last Task: Using the Station to Lobby Congress for More Money

ONE OF DR. HASTINGS'S last tasks was to accompany Astoria's politically influential Judge Bowlby on a tour of the newly opened station. This was not just any visit. In March, Bowlby was appointed to Astoria's Chamber of Commerce "Commerce and Navigation Committee." He became one of several regional and national politicians attempting to obtain new federal and state money for the area around the mouth of the river. It was to pay for an expansion of the river's commercial use. Even Portland's Chamber of Commerce participated, asking for $2.5 million.[191]

After Bowlby and Hastings toured the station, the judge wrote a newspaper article describing the station in such a way that it solicited more money.[192]

> *One house on the shore has been built for the accommodation of the employee. The old Knapp dwelling, if worth rejuvenating, may be fitted up for the occupation of the officers of the ship quarantined. There... besides these a barracks on shore for the accommodation of all passengers. All these launching items will require about the approximate sum of*

[191] LOC, *Morning Astorian*, December 13, 1900, image.
[192] *ADB* , March 14, 1900, "About the City."

$65,000. The original appropriation of $30,000 is exhausted. Spent has been $8,000 for the site, wharf $10,000 and machinery $5,000.

On December 11th Judge Bowlby reported an "urgent need for further buildings to make the plant complete." An additional $60,000 was needed. And yet, he also stated that [193] "it has been constructed and completed and unquestionable is one of the best equipped."[194]

On the same day, Dr. Hastings performed a last administrative act when he added Joe Johnson to the payroll as a temporary attendant. His wage would be $2.50 per day.[195] Like Anne Abraham, he lived with his sister a few hundred yards from the station.

Hastings was on the way to California by mid-December, taking the railroad. He looked forward to working in a warmer climate that promised to be better for his health. Dr. Hayworth Baylis Earle took over as the new master of the USPHS quarantine station with a flying start and without problems. Dr. Hastings and Dr. Earle met in Astoria a few years later one more time for a social visit. Hill Hastings never looked back. He found an entirely new life in California. He would leave the USPHS and become an administrator of a medical school.

Astoria's bar pilots and the shipping community, in general, did look back once in a while. Then Dr. Hastings was mentioned as somebody who performed his work above average with a sense of fairness and commitment to institutional professionalism that needs to be retaught every generation. Yes, he had not been beloved socially. Nevertheless, he established the dominance of national public health rules while keeping commerce running. That was understood as making possible the income of lots of money from the 1900 salmon harvests as well as wheat and wood exports across the globe.

193 LOC, *Morning Astorian*, December 13, 1900.
194 LOC, *Morning Astorian*, November 24, 1900.
195 NARA, RG 90, Earle to D.C. December 31, 1900.

While Oregon weather and Astoria were not his favorites, Dr. Hastings's work should be remembered above others. Not only did he build the station that all others would use after him. There would never be a complaint about the quality of the new construction he supervised. More importantly, he did it under the very real threat of plague establishing itself in Astoria and along the Columbia River without much federal help. His greatest present was not to panic.

Sources

Libraries and Archives

Appelo Archive Center, Naselle, WA.
Astoria Public Library, Astoria, OR.
  Newspaper Collection.
Clatsop County Historical Society, Astoria, OR.
  Liisa Penner Research Center and Archives.
Columbia River Maritime Museum, Astoria, OR.
Keck School of Medicine of USC, Los Angeles, CA,
  Online Collections.
Library of Congress, Washington D.C.
National Archives and Records Administration (NARA), Seattle, WA
  Collection Government Surplus Records.
National Archives and Records Administration (NARA), Washington, D.C.
  Records of the Department of Treasury.
  Records of the Department of Commerce.
  Records of the United States Public Health Service.
  Census Records.
  Passport Applications.
National Library of Medicine
  Archives and Personal Papers Collections.
    Association of Military Surgeons of the United States Biographical Sketch
    Kinyoun, Joseph J. Papers. https://resource.nlm.nih.gov/9803039.
  Images from the History of Medicine Collection.
Oregon Historical Society, Portland, OR.
Pacific County Historical Society, South Bend, WA,
San Francisco Public Library, San Francisco, CA.
Islapedia: https://www.islapedia.com/.
Wikimedia Commons; https://commons.wikimedia.org.
Ancestry; https://www.ancestry.com.

Secondary Sources

Chronicling America: Historic American Newspapers. Library of Congress, https://chroniclingamerica.loc.gov/.

Publications from the U.S. Department of Health & Human Services

Frankfurter Allgemeine Zeitung (Frankfurt General Newspaper) Frankfurt, Germany, https://www.faz.net/.

Books

Anderson, Nancy Bell, and Heather Bell Henry. *The Columbia River's "Ellis Island": The Story of Knappton Cove.* Gearhart, OR: Heritage Folk Press, 2012.

Appelo, Carlton E., *Knappton the first 50 years, Pacific County, Washington.* Self-published, Deep River, Washington, 1975.

Astoria Bicentennial Committee. *Astoria 1811-2011: An Adventure in History, Bicentennial Celebration, Official Commemorative Program.* Astoria, OR: Clatsop County Historical Society, 2011.

Burmester, Heinz, Uwe Jarchow, and Walter Kresse. *Grossegler Rickmer Rickmers: Seine Wechselvolle Geschichte* [Tall Ship Rickmer Rickmers: Its Eventful History]. Hamburg: Ernst Kabel Verlag, 1986.

Echenberg, Myron. *Plague Ports: The Global Urban Impact Of Bubonic Plague, 1894–1901.* New York: NYU Press, 2007.

Kirtley, Karen, ed. *Astorians: Eccentric and Extraordinary.* Salem OR: Eastern Oregonian Pub. Co.; Corvallis, OR: Distributed by Oregon State University Press, 2010.

Martin, Irene and Roger Tetlow. *Flight of the Bumble Bee: The Columbia River Packers Association & a Century in the Pursuit of Fish.* Long Beach, WA: The Chinook Observer, 2011.

Riese, B. Guenter, *Plague, Fear and Politics in San Francisco's Chinatown,* Baltimore: John Hopkins University Press, 2012.

Articles

Kramer, George. *Grain, Flower and Ships: The Wheat Trade in Portland, Oregon.* Heritage Research Associates Report No. 448 prepared for Prosper Portland, April 2019, https://docslib.org/doc/597271/grain-flour-and-ships-the-wheat-trade-in-portland-oregon

Image Credits

x .... Courtesy of the Clatsop County Historical Society, (hereafter cited as CCHS)
2 .... Keck School of Medicine, University of Southern California
8 .... CCHS, Sanborn Insurance Map
12 .... Clatsop County Historical Society
14 .... National Library of Medicine (hereafter cited as NLM)
18 .... CCHS
20 .... CCHS
22 .... Library of Congress (hereafter cited as LOC)
26 .... Washington Rural Heritage, Skamania County Heritage
28 .... National Archives and Records Administration (hereafter cited as NARA), Washington, D.C.
30 .... LOC
32 .... Astoria Public Library, *Astoria Daily Budget*
34 .... CCHS
36 .... Appelo Research Center, Naselle, WA.
38 .... NARA, Seattle, WA.
42 .... Hawaii State Archives Digital Collection
46 .... LOC
48 .... NLM, digital collecction
50 .... NARA, Washington D. C.
52 .... NARA, Washington D.C.
54 .... NARA, Seattle, WA.
56 .... CCHS
58 .... CCHS
58 .... CCHS
66 .... NLM
68 .... LOC
70 .... CCHS
72 .... NARA, Washington, D.C.

76 .... LOC
78 .... ISLAPEDIA
80 .... NLM
82 .... CCHS
84 .... LOC
86 .... LOC
88 .... SAN FRANCISCO PUBLIC LIBRARY
90 .... NARA, WASHINGTON, D.C.
92 .... LOC
94 .... NLM
98 .... CCHS
100 .... WIKIMEDIA COMMONS
102 .... NARA, WASHINGTON, D.C.
106 .... ASTORIA PUBLIC LIBRARY
108 .... NARA, SEATTLE, WA.
110 .... COLUMBIA RIVER MARITIME MUSEUM (HEREAFTER CITED AS CRMM)
112 .... APPELO ARCHIVES CENTER, NASELLE, WA.
114 .... CCHS
116 .... NARA, WASHINGTON, D.C.
118 .... NARA, WASHINGTON, D.C.
120 .... CCHS
122 .... CRMM
124 .... NLM

www.ingramcontent.com/pod-product-compliance
Ingram Content Group UK Ltd.
Pitfield, Milton Keynes, MK11 3LW, UK
UKHW062311290726
14090UKWH00018B/1012

9 798218 132507